THE PRACTICAL GUIDE TO GUNS AND SHOOTING

HANDGUN EDITION

TOM MCHALE

IPG PRESS

I'd like to dedicate this book to my wife and best friend of many years. I couldn't ask for a more dedicated and supportive partner in these endeavors.

"A wife of noble character who can find? She is worth far more than rubies. Her husband has full confidence in her and lacks nothing of value. She brings him good, not harm, all the days of her life."
Proverbs 31:10-12

BUT FIRST, A SERIOUS NOTE

PROPER HANDLING and carrying of firearms is serious business. While we aim (Ha! Pun intended!) to make the shooting world more accessible and understandable with a little humor now and then, we firmly believe that nothing takes the place of face-to-face, real-time training. So use this guide as an educational tool to help you understand some of the basics, but never substitute the contents of a publication like this one for the expert advice of a skilled and experienced firearms and personal defense trainer.

One more safety note. Before you handle any guns, review the rules of Gun Safety chapter in this book. They're simple and obvious, but if you obey them faithfully no one can ever get hurt.

Now back to business.

Although this is the Handgun Edition, we'll talk just a bit about rifles and shotguns for clarification in some of the crossover areas. In the not too distant future, look for more Practical Guides that are specific to rifles, shotguns and shooting accessories.

In true MyGunCulture.com style, this book is written in literary assault format for your enjoyment — half-cocked but right on target. I hope that doesn't offend your sense of decency and decorum — too much.

PART I

HANDGUNS AND HOW THEY WORK

When you boil down all the terminology, details, and design features, guns are pretty simple things. They fling projectiles, called bullets, forward at high velocity in order to make holes.

All guns do this. Where they differ is in the details of their size, operation, and the type of projectiles they fire. Handguns are just pint-sized guns designed to be fired with one hand if necessary. I've always thought that handguns should really be called "hand-s-guns" because in an ideal situation, they're more effective when operated with both hands, but that's another story.

In this section we're going to explore different types of handguns. Handguns come in many styles: semi-automatic pistols, revolvers, derringers or single shot models just to name a few. We'll also spend a bit of time discussing different "actions." Like manual and automatic transmission cars, handguns have different operating modes too. Understanding the pros and cons of different styles will be important when it comes time to choose one to fit your needs and preferences.

For comparison, we'll also very briefly outline the difference between handguns, rifles, and shotguns.

Now, let's get started!

PISTOLS

These Smith & Wesson M&P handguns are both pistols.

A PISTOL IS A VERY specific type of handgun, not just a general term for one. In simple terms, pistols are (usually) the type of handguns that store extra rounds of ammunition in the grip. Take a look at your nearest law enforcement officer; odds are that they are carrying a pistol.

If we get really nitpicky, we would define "pistol" as a handgun that has its chamber integral with the barrel. Right off the bat, that leads us to the technical definition of "chamber." A quick diversion on that topic is warranted; we'll use that word a lot throughout the book.

Chamber

You can think of the chamber of a gun as the very back part of the barrel, where a cartridge is placed and ready to fire. As with all this complicated gun stuff, a chamber is not always the same as the back of the barrel. Revolvers have chambers that are separate from the barrel. They still hold the cartridge in place to fire. However, revolver chambers line up with the back of the barrel when ready to fire.

The chambers of a revolver (left) aren't attached to the barrel, while the chamber of a pistol (right) is part of the barrel itself.

So technically, a pistol could be a single shot pistol, a derringer or perhaps a semi-automatic pistol like the Glocks that most law enforcement officers carry. For purposes of this book, we're going to use the word pistol primarily to describe semi-automatic pistols like the ones shown above. If we talk about other types of pistols, like single shots and derringers, we'll be sure to specify.

We've mentioned "semi-automatic pistols" so we ought to spend just a second specifying what those are. Semi-automatic simply indicates that the gun does part of the work for you. It's not fully automatic, meaning that it doesn't shoot multiple times with one pull of the trigger. Get it? Semi as in "part," and automatic as in "you don't have to do all the work."

Many guns use some of the energy from a firing cartridge to eject the empty cartridge shell and load a new one for you. The "semi" part of a semi-automatic is important here because you, the shooter, still have to operate the gun for each and every shot. When you press the trigger, it only fires one time and one time only. All that's automated is the ejection of the spent cartridge case and loading of the next cartridge into the chamber. You can think of a semi-automatic handgun design kind of like of like an electric staple gun. You have to press the go switch to staple something; it just gets it ready to go for you. Or you could think of semi-automatic kind of like politicians and TV cameras. When you make a deliberate action to turn on a TV camera, a politician will automatically reload right in front of it.

Most semi-automatic pistols are pretty similar at first glance. Modern ones generally have a magazine in the grip that holds the cartridges and prepares them for loading into the chamber. So, unlike a revolver, a pistol arranges extra cartridges vertically. As the gun is fired, a spring in the magazine pushes the stack of cartridges upwards towards the chamber.

Folks who favor semi-automatic pistols like them for many reasons.

- Semi-automatic pistols generally have more cartridge capacity than revolvers. This simply means they hold more bullets and you don't have to reload it as often. Many modern pistols can hold up to 20 cartridges in the magazine.
- Pistols are easier and faster to reload than revolvers. To reload a pistol, the user simply activates a button or lever to release the empty magazine. Then you insert a full one.

- Semi-automatic pistols may appear to have less recoil — all else being equal. While physics is physics and the overall recoil force is the same, some of the recoil energy is directed towards the semi-automatic operation of the pistol. So many shooters report "feeling" less recoil with a semi-automatic pistol than a comparably powered revolver.

If you talk to a couple of gun aficionados, you're likely to hear about what sounds like yet another type of handgun — the 1911. No worries, it's just a type of semi-automatic pistol. People tend to get pretty passionate about 1911 style pistols, so they tend to get placed in their own category.

1911 Pistols

You'll hear gun folks talk in reverential tones about something called a 1911. Yes, it's a year. It also sounds a little bit like a famous model of Porsche. But in context of this book, it's a pistol design. Not a manufacturer or a specific model, but a design. Kind of like how a pickup truck is a design. Lot's of car manufacturers make them, and you can get them with different size engines, but they all have some common features, like seats in the front and a cargo bed in the back.

It's not a perfect analogy, but 1911's are kind of like pickup trucks. They are all based on a semi-automatic pistol design, invented and brought to market in, you guessed it, the year 1911 by one John Moses Browning — may God rest his soul. 1911's have some common design elements, regardless of which manufacturer makes them and often parts are interchangeable. For example, classic 1911's are all single-action semi-automatics, have a thumb and grip safety, and a similar design to lock and unlock the barrel during recoil.

Listening to 1911 fans, you might believe that they're invincible. They have been known to take down both a Japanese Zero fighter and German Storch observation plane in World War II. In fact, some believe that a stray 1911 .45 ACP round inadvertently destroyed the city of Dresden. OK, the Dresden thing may be a slight exaggeration, but the 1911 has been a phenomenally successful and long-lived design, and the classic version fires a large bullet as far as handguns go.

There are different types of semi-automatic pistols, and since you'll hear about some of these at gun stores, shows, and ranges, we'll take a look at three major types later in this chapter: single-action, double-action and striker-fired.

Here's an assortment of Smith & Wesson 1911s. They're a "class" of pistols with similar design features.

We're not going to get too wrapped up in the specifics of proper gun terminology. It can be intimidating and quite frankly, it's not all that important as long as people know what you're trying to say. But we will try to be accurate so you have the full picture.

Right off the bat, we're going to run into a problematic situation. You see, some gun folks are so darn persnickety about using the correct words that someone, somewhere, is bound to correct you on your use of a gun word. Maybe you'll walk into a gun store and ask if they carry extra clips for your Springfield XD handgun. Or perhaps you'll refer to your Smith & Wesson 642 Airweight revolver as a "pistol". Do they know what you mean? Yes. Is it really necessary to cop an attitude and correct you? No.

Magazines and Clips

You know how you can spot a high school prom couple at an exclusive restaurant? Like when the pimply mannish boy requests A-1 Steak Sauce with his Chateaubriand? Well, there's a similar thing in shooting – when people carelessly throw around words like clip.

Clips and magazines are both legitimate shooting related objects. While sometimes subtle, there are differences.

A clip is a device used to hold cartridges for the purpose of storage, packing, and easy loading into a magazine. Clips were a big deal back when the world had anger issues expressed by frequent large-scale wars. Five or ten rounds of ammo might be attached to a clip, which would allow a soldier to slide the rounds into the magazine of his rifle or handgun quickly and easily. Clips are still used today. Some .223 or 5.56 ammunition comes on clips to make it easier to load lots of rounds into a magazine at once.

A magazine is a container that holds cartridges to feed them into the chamber of a firearm. Magazines can be built into the gun, as with many rifles, or they can be removable, as with most semi-automatic pistols and AR type rifles. That thing that falls out the bottom of a Glock? That's a magazine.

Confused? No problem. We've got a near fail-safe tip for you. These days you're pretty safe referring to most things that hold bullets as a magazine. More often than not, you'll be correct referring to it that way.

While the shooting industry is starting to get pretty good at traditional retail things like civility and customer service, you'll still run into the occasional Clems who might look down their nose at new shooters. Ignore them and move on. Because you'll find that, overwhelmingly, the shooting community is full of really nice and respectable folks that want to help. Try us on this. Go to a big match to watch. And you'll see things like the industry's most famous professionals stop to ask if you need help. Other shooters will ask if you need to borrow a gun or ammunition. 95% of the youth in attendance will refer to you as "maam" or "sir."

So don't get too hung up on exact terminology. And by all means, don't let that be a barrier to your participation! We know what you mean after all!

With all that said, we're going to point out correct terminology for specific things in this book, just so you know, but don't get too worked up about it. Shooting sports are supposed to be fun.

This Springfield Armory XD-E uses a magazine to hold cartridges in the grip.

GUN WORDS EXPLAINED

Caliber [kal-uh-ber]

- Noun

1. The interior diameter of the bore of a gun barrel, usually measured in inches or millimeters.

A gun barrel with an interior diameter of .357 inches in diameter is technically .357 caliber. Caliber measures the diameter of the bullet and has nothing to do with length or weight of the actual bullet, although calibers have taken on broader meaning in casual conversation. If someone refers to a caliber of 9mm, then they are really talking about a 9mm Luger cartridge and all the assumptions that go with that.

2. A sinister plot by gun people to make things extra-confusing for new shooters.

For example, .38 caliber really means .357 inches in diameter and .380 caliber really means .355 inches in diameter. 9 millimeter also means .355 inches in diameter. To keep things plenty confusing, .40 caliber really does mean .40 inches in diameter. Same with .45 caliber — that means .45 inches.

However, .44 caliber really means .430 inches. Of course, .32 ACP (caliber) really means .312 inches. .30 caliber rifle bullets are particularly easy. Some are .308 inches and others are .311 inches. Got all that? See, isn't this gun stuff easy?

In a minute, we'll talk about two types of revolvers, double-action and single-action.

REVOLVERS

Here's a Smith & Wesson 586 L-Comp revolver chambered in .357 Magnum.

REVOLVERS ARE easy to master from a terminology standpoint.

According to the Urban Dictionary, Revolver is the Beatles greatest album and was released in 1966. That doesn't really help much unless you're learning to shoot with Sgt. Pepper's Lonely Hearts Club Band. So we can turn to Dictionary.com and see that the verb "revolve" means to turn around or rotate, as on an axis. That's more helpful!

All revolvers have multiple chambers arranged in a cylinder. The cylinder rotates in order to line up each chamber with the barrel when it's ready to fire. Simple right? If you see a handgun that has a round cylinder, you've got an excellent chance of identifying it correctly as a revolver!

Some folks prefer revolvers because they are simple and reliable.

- As the chambers are all in the cylinder, it's very easy to check if a revolver is loaded or unloaded because you can see the entire cylinder and its contents at once. But remember, a gun is always loaded!
- Double-action revolvers are simple to operate. Just pull the trigger and it will fire. There are no external safeties or magazine operations to worry about.
- A single-action revolver is a great gun for new shooters as it's very deliberate. To fire a shot, you have to first cock the hammer, then pull the trigger.
- While there are exceptions, most revolvers can hold between 5 and 8 cartridges in a cylinder. Some small caliber revolvers can hold more than 8.

OTHER TYPES OF HANDGUNS

Single Shot

WE'RE NOT GOING to spend a lot of time on single-shot handguns as the name pretty much sums things up.

Single-shot handguns fire once.

Then you have to reload them.

This is a Thompson Center single-shot handgun. It's generally used for hunting and target shooting.

Modern single-shot handguns are generally used for hunting and firing unusual calibers. Like the modern derringer, many feature interchangeable barrels. You might hear of "Thompson Center" handguns. These are a great example of a modern single shot handgun. The action breaks open so that the chamber is exposed. This allows loading of a single cartridge.

Derringers

Even though the word "derringer" sounds French, it still manages to sound tough doesn't it?

Technically, a derringer is a pocket pistol, and for any given caliber, it's about as small a gun as you can get. Derringers typically are designed to fire single shots and are very simple mechanically. This simplicity allows them to be very small.

Modern derringers like this Bond Arms model have interchangeable barrels so you can choose different calibers.

Original derringers were single shot muzzle loaders — you know, like the pistols in Pirates of the Caribbean, only much, much smaller. Modern derringers tend to have two barrels, with each loaded with a single cartridge. Even though many modern derringers can fire two shots, it's not because they have a repeating action. They just have two single shot barrels duct taped together. Well, only the really cheap ones are duct taped. Higher quality models use staples. Nah, still kidding. Modern derringers are actually really nice guns that are the pocket gun equivalent of a nice over and under shotgun with two barrels carefully machined or welded together.

Because the history of derringers is such as fascinating tale, we're going to take a quick diversion here.

A Brief History of The Derringer

Coincidentally, the derringer pistol was invented by an American gunsmith named Henry Deringer. Yes, that's Deringer with one "r." Imagine the odds of that! But back to the story. Deringer ran a thriving business in Philadelphia, manufacturing Model 1814 and 1817 Common Rifles for military contracts. Of course, the real cash cow for Deringer's business was running guided tours of Rocky V film locations.

Back to guns. Deringer was famous for his small pistol designs, which were all single shot muzzle loaders, usually of large-caliber. In

1852, he started making the pistols pocket-sized and they became known as derringers — with two "R's." Why the public added that second "R" remains a mystery. Henry Deringer did not think of his derringer pistol as anything particularly noteworthy and therefore never patented his invention. As a result, Henry died leaving only a modest estate and was never invited to ring the opening bell at the New York Stock Exchange.

As the derringer gained in popularity, specific designs of derringers for women, called hand muff pistols, became fashionable. No, we're not making this up. Hand muff pistols were popular as the small derringer could easily fit in hand muffs, thereby offering concealment and quick access should an urgent self-defense need arise.

HANDGUN ACTIONS

WHILE WE'RE HERE DEFINING handguns, we need to discuss some action.

We've already covered **types** of handguns (like pistols and revolvers) but now we need to talk for a minute about types of action. And when I say, "action", I'm talking about the method of operation of that handgun. It gets a bit complicated as both pistols and revolvers can have the same "type" of action.

- You can have a single-action revolver.
- You can have a single-action pistol.
- You can have a double-action pistol
- You can have a double-action revolver.
- You can have a striker-fired pistol.
- But you can't have a striker-fired revolver — that I know of.

Let's dive into how the different action types work. We'll also touch on some of the pros and cons to help you decide what might work best for you.

Single-Action

Single-action is a pretty simple concept. And it has nothing to do with online dating sites, chance encounters at the laundromat or a night on the town with two wild and crazy guys.

When a handgun is single-action, whether it's a pistol or revolver, it does one thing (or action) when you pull the trigger. The descriptor, single-action, must be entirely coincidental right?

Both of these handguns are single-action designs. Note the cocked hammer on each.

While I'm sure there's an exception out there, in most cases, pressing the trigger of a single-action gun will release a hammer, allowing it to strike a firing pin that whacks the back of a cartridge and ignites it. So, pressing the trigger does one action — which results in firing the gun.

Here's a pair of Ruger revolvers. The one on the upper left is a single-action model while the bottom one is a double-action.

Here's where it gets tricky. Some single-action guns need to be manually cocked between each shot. Perhaps the best example of this is the traditional cowboy six gun, commonly called a single-action revolver. The shooter must "cock the hammer" to prepare it for that single-action release by a trigger press. In old western movies, this is done really fast — sometimes with the shooter smacking the hammer with one hand while holding the trigger down with the other. That technique is **not recommended** by the way.

Hammer [ham-er]

- *Noun*

1. The part of a firearm designed to impart mechanical energy to the firing pin in order to strike the primer of a cartridge. Some hammers, such as those on older revolvers, have the firing pin attached to the hammer and directly impact the primer. Others, generally on more modern designs, impact a transfer bar or mechanism to provide energy to the firing pin. The hammer of a gun does not have to be exposed or visible. For example, the Smith and Wesson 642 revolver and M1 Garand semi-automatic rifle both have internal hammers.

2. Easily confused with similar terms. For example, "*Hammer Time*" is not an appropriate usage in the context of guns, unless you've got slick moves and a pair of parachute pants capable of providing wind power for the city of San Francisco. Otherwise, you can't touch this.

However, not all single-action handguns have to be manually cocked between each shot. Some single-action designs, like the 1911 pistol, are manually cocked for the first shot. Each subsequent shot uses the recoil action to automatically cock the hammer for the next shot. Since the trigger still does only one thing, release the hammer, these guns are still considered single-actions. Make sense?

So what's the big deal about single action?

Generally speaking — I'll bet a nickel someone will find an exception — single-action guns have relatively "light" triggers since the trigger only serves to release the hammer. A "light" trigger doesn't require a lot of pressure to activate. A "light" trigger press makes for a gun that is easier to shoot accurately. It's not mechanically more accurate; it's just easier to shoot accurately. This is because the force of your finger is less likely to pull the sights off target. If it takes eight pounds of pressure to press the trigger, and the gun only weighs three pounds, then the shooter really has to concentrate to keep that gun perfectly still during a trigger press. On the other hand, if the trigger press requires two pounds, and the gun weighs three pounds, then the shooter is less likely to pull the gun off target while pressing the trigger.

So, all of that is a fancy way of saying that many folks like single-action guns because they can be easy to shoot accurately.

There's a lot more to consider when deciding whether to use a single-action gun, so for now, let's just stick to the definitions. We'll talk about pros and cons later.

Double-Action

Double-action is not a dirty word, so get that out of your head.

Double-action simply means that the trigger press motion can accomplish not one, but two, distinct actions. A double-action gun can use the trigger press to both cock the hammer and release it to fire. So, with a double-action gun, you don't (necessarily) need to cock the hammer in order to fire the gun. A trigger press can accomplish both actions.

By necessity, and those pesky laws of physics (Dang that Newton guy!), a double-action gun requires more force to operate the trigger. That's because the trigger is cocking and releasing the hammer or striker. It does more work, so it requires more energy on your part. There's no such thing as a free lunch.

Here's the part where we start talking about complications and exceptions. You knew that was coming, right?

One of the benefits of most double-action guns is that they can operate in either double-action or single-action mode. Technically, you could refer to these as DA/SA (double-action/single-action) guns. For purposes of simplicity, we'll just call them double-action. Just be aware there are some double-action pistols that have no single-action mode.

This Smith & Wesson revolver is a double-action that can also be fired in single-action mode by manually cocking the hammer.

To illustrate this point, lets look at a really common double-action pistol — the Beretta 92FS. This is the civilian version of the standard pistol that United States military men and women use.

The Beretta 92FS is a classic double-action pistol design. Once a cartridge is loaded in the chamber, there are two ways to fire the pistol. Method one is to simply pull the trigger, making sure the safety lever is off first. You'll notice that the trigger requires a longer press, with more pressure, to fire the shot. That's because as you press the trigger, the hammer is raised into the firing position. As you continue to press the trigger, the hammer is released, and the shot is fired.

Things get interesting after the first shot. Most double-action pistols (not revolvers) use some of the recoil energy from each shot to eject the spent cartridge casing, load a new cartridge and most importantly to this discussion, cock the hammer or striker. So, for subsequent shots, the pistol operates in single-action mode. Got that? The hammer is already cocked, so pressing the trigger does one thing (single-action) and that is releasing the hammer to fire the cartridge.

To sum it up, with double-action pistols, the first shot requires a longer, more forceful, trigger press to operate in double-action mode. Each subsequent shot operates in single-action with a shorter and lighter trigger press since the hammer is cocked automatically.

Revolvers with exposed hammers work a little bit differently. You can press the trigger in double-action mode to cock the hammer and release it to fire the shot. You can also manually cock the hammer and fire the revolver in single-action mode. The difference lies in how the subsequent shots operate. With a double-action pistol, recoil energy is used to eject a spent cartridge, load a new one and cock the hammer. Revolvers have none of this. So, for the second shot with a revolver, the shooter is faced with a choice to shoot double-action again, or to manually cock the hammer and shoot single-action.

Both of these are double-action handguns. A Beretta PX4 Storm .40 S&W caliber (above) and a Ruger LCR .357 revolver (below).

Some double-action revolvers do not have an exposed hammer, like the Ruger LCR shown here. Since there is no way to manually cock the hammer, each shot is fired in double-action mode.

So what's the big deal with double-action pistols?

The advantage of the double-action design is safety. Since the first trigger press requires a forceful and deliberate effort to cock the hammer and fire the gun,

This Ruger LCR is a double-action revolver. You just can't see the hammer because it's inside of the frame.

the shooter really has to intend to fire. An accidental finger twitch is less likely to result in an unplanned shot. There's some merit to the idea that in a high-stress situation like self-defense or law enforcement duties you don't want a trigger that's too easy to activate. On the other hand, remember that it's harder to shoot accurately when the trigger press requires more pressure.

The primary disadvantage is the difference in feel between first and second shots. With double-action / single-action pistols, the first shot will require a longer and hard trigger press. Subsequent shots will require a lighter and shorter press. Acclimating a shooter to account for the difference, under stress, requires training and practice.

So what do you do?

Try it for yourself. My collection has both single-action and double-action pistols and revolvers. I personally don't mind shooting double-action pistols like the Beretta 92. But then again, I like to shoot frequently and I practice. I don't really notice that transition between single and double-action. If you are realistically not going to practice on a regular basis, you may want to consider a design with fewer variables like a double-action only revolver or striker-fired pistol. We'll talk about those next.

Striker-Fired

Striker-fired pistols are a little ambiguous, and just to muddy the waters, there's a lot of confusion between which pistols are double-action, single-action and striker-fired. Some double-action / single-action pistols use a striker instead of a hammer. For purposes of simplicity — you're not believing the whole guns and simplicity thing are you? — we'll neglect those as we define striker-fired guns here.

First, let's define what striker-fired means, more or less.

While there will be more exceptions than visitors to a Jersey Shore spray tan salon, we'll refer to striker-fired guns as those with existing tension on the striker bar. Think of it this way. In a hammer fired gun, there may be a spring between the firing pin and the cartridge. This spring prevents the striker or firing pin from hitting the cartridge until some external force, like the hammer, overcomes the pressure of the spring and forces the striker to hit the cartridge primer. In a striker-fired gun, the spring could be **behind** the striker or firing pin. This means that constant pressure is being applied to the striker, encouraging it to move towards the cartridge primer and fire the gun. An internal part called a sear prevents this motion until the trigger is pressed. A sear is simply a piece of metal that holds the hammer or striker in place until enough pressure is applied to the trigger.

Does that makes sense? In a double-action or single-action scenario (generally speaking) there is pressure keeping the striker or firing pin separated from the live cartridge until a hammer is released to overcome that pressure. In a striker-fired situation, there is constant pressure on the striker towards the cartridge. The sear prevents the striker from releasing until the trigger is pressed.

This Sig Sauer P320 is a striker-fired pistol. Look, no hammer!

If we were to get into the gory details, there's a bit more to the story. For example, most striker-fired guns maintain the striker in "partially" ready position. The trigger pull applies the rest of the tension necessary to complete a strike on the cartridge. This is one of the reasons that the lines between single, double-action and striker-fired designs are so blurry, but that's not relevant to our discussion here, so we'll move on.

This discussion of fire-control system engineering is all good and nice, but how is it relevant to choosing a gun that's right for you? Let's look at some real world pros and cons of striker-fired designs versus single and double-action designs.

So what's the big deal about striker-fired pistols?

Most striker-fired pistols offer a constant trigger pull from first to last shot. If you've been paying attention to all this mumbo-jumbo, you know that you can achieve constant, first to last shot, trigger pull with a double-action gun. Aha! You're right! But with a striker-fired gun, some of the pressure required to strike the firing pin exists before you start to pull the trigger. This means that a striker-fired gun can have a lighter trigger pull than a double-action gun, yet still offer the same trigger press weight for all shots. For the first shot, the gun is partially cocked with the initial act of chambering a cartridge. Each subsequent shot also partially cocks the gun. So, the trigger pull simply completes the cocking process, then releases the firing pin.

So the net-net of all this technical discussion? A striker-fired gun "acts" like a double-action gun where each trigger pull is the same. It also has a heavier trigger pull than a single-action gun, which provides more margin of safety against unintended discharges. But many think it's a lot easier to shoot well than a double-action gun with a heavier trigger pull.

What does a striker-fired handgun look like? A Glock. Of course, many other modern pistols are striker-fired. Like the Smith & Wesson M&P and the Springfield Armory XD. There are lots of others of course. The point is that striker-fired guns have become popular for the reasons stated here. When was the last time you saw a law enforcement officer of any type? The odds are 86.327% in favor of them carrying a striker-fired gun.

That's enough about handgun action types. That stuff is exhausting.

OTHER TYPES OF GUNS

THIS BOOK IS PRIMARILY about handguns but for clarity let's briefly touch on rifles and shotguns.

Rifles

This is the Practical Guide to Guns and Shooting, so we're not going to get wrapped up in obscure technical differences between rifles and smoothbores. After all, the objective is to communicate information you need to know in order to survive and thrive on your next visit to a gun store, range or shooting club.

With that said, we're going to use two defining characteristics to explain what a rifle is.

First, a rifle is not a handgun. It's longer. And a rifle is generally intended to be fired using both hands and a shoulder for support. For obvious reasons, many people refer to rifles as long guns. Yes, really. Gun stuff is not always overly complex.

Second, a rifle has rifling. I know, that sounds like an epiphany from the Psychic Hotline. But it's true.

Rifling

Simply put, rifling refers to the interior surface shape of a gun barrel. Through a variety of techniques, grooves are cut or pressed into the interior of the bore. These grooves are shaped in a spiral pattern, like those DNA strand pictures you saw in high school chemistry. With its rifling grooves, a gun barrel is just a gnats hair smaller in diameter than the bullet that it is intended to fire. So as a bullet is forced through the barrel, the rifling grabs the bullet and imparts spin. Think about throwing a football. If you just toss it without spiraling the ball, it won't go very fast or far and will probably miss your target. Not only does a ball fly with more stability and accuracy while spinning, the motion also keeps one of the pointy ends facing forward. That's why it can fly farther and faster. In contrast, imagine a quarterback throwing a football while wearing a baseball glove. He can apply the same amount of force, but his passes wouldn't be helping his Hall of Fame aspirations. That might resemble trying to throw a live turkey.

We customized this Ruger 10/22 rifle for a charity benefit. It's a great example of a modern .22 target rifle.

Rifles come in all shapes and sizes for different purposes. You can even buy them at many Wal-Marts as they are common tools for hunting, home defense and recreation. Mostly, they vary by the type of action they use. Some common types include semi-automatic, lever-action, bolt-action, single-shot and pump-action.

Assault Weapons

There's no such thing as an "assault weapon." Next topic.

OK. there **is** such a thing as an assault rifle. That specific term generally refers to a military rifle that is capable of firing in full-automatic mode. That means that the rifle will keep shooting as long as the trigger is held down, until it runs out of ammunition. Ever see the movie Predator? Most of the guns in the movie **are** actually assault rifles — not assault weapons!

There's a lot of confusion, misunderstanding, and downright lies about "assault weapons," so let's clarify what's what.

Actual assault rifles are illegal for practical purposes. Law enforcement and military organizations can buy new ones off the shelf, but that's it. Civilians can, under very difficult and expensive circumstances, acquire an assault rifle provided it was made prior to 1986. Since there's a very limited supply, actual assault rifles are incredible expensive, ranging from $20,000 well into the six-figure range. And it's not just the money that's a barrier. You'll need to apply to the Bureau of Alcohol, Tobacco, Firearms, and Explosives for a special Class III permit, undergo all sorts of background checks, fingerprints and other approval. If and when you get approved, all that applies to only a single gun. Oh, and if you want to move it across state lines, you'll be subject to more paperwork and approvals.

So, for practical purposes, real assault rifles (fully automatic "machine" guns) have been banned for a long time.

"Assault weapon" is a made-up term. That's not an exaggeration. There really is no such thing as an "assault weapon." Politicians past and present have and continue to enact laws that restrict rifles that they deem dangerous, but since fully automatic rifles are already banned, they've defined "assault weapons" by cosmetic features. While state laws vary, some "assault weapons" are defined by presence of things like a flash hider muzzle device, adjustable stock, pistol-style grip, or bayonet lug. There are no functional differences between a regular semi-automatic rifle and a so-called "assault weapon" other than these cosmetic differences.

Doesn't make much sense does it? That's exactly the outcome desired by proponents of the term "assault weapon." It's a term engineered to confuse people and it's been shockingly effective in that mission.

Shotguns

As you're probably already figuring out, guns and their related terms are intended to be understood only by wayward monks strung out on peyote. So recognizing that anything in the world of guns and shooting has exceptions, let's take a crack at a simple definition of a shotgun.

A shotgun has two primary characteristics. Mostly.

1. They fire "shells" that usually contain multiple spherical projectiles.
2. Unlike handguns and rifles, they have smooth, not rifled barrels.

While some companies make handguns that fire smaller shotgun shells, most shotguns are intended to be shoulder-fired. So at first glance, they resemble rifles. However, since they fire multiple projectiles with each shot, they tend to be better suited for hitting close-range moving objects — like birds or clay targets. The interior of a shotgun barrel is (generally) not rifled as rifling would impart spin on the column of pellets as they move down the barrel and this would cause the pellets to disperse too widely upon leaving the muzzle.

Shotguns comes in all types. From top to bottom: A Browning BPS pump-action 12-gauge, a Browning Gold Fusion semi-automatic 12-gauge and a Winchester 9410 .410 lever-action.

Shotgun ammunition is generally composed of multiple projectiles in a single cartridge, or "shell" if you want to be technical. Here's an easy way to visualize how shotguns work. Imagine chunking a rock at a squirrel that keeps raiding your bird feeder. If you throw one rock at that gluttonous little bugger, that's kinda like using a "normal" handgun or rifle. You have to aim that single rock pretty carefully. But on the plus side, you can throw it pretty far as all of your arm strength is focused on that one rock. If you pick up a handful of rocks, and throw them all at once, that's kind of like a shotgun. You might stand a little better chance of hitting your irreverent squirrel at short distances, but he's not going to be quite as aggravated as if he was bonked with a single, well-aimed stone. That's because your throwing strength is spread out across all of the rocks. Each one get's a fraction of the power generated by your bicep and tricep guns. Make sense?

The shot (or rocks in our example) in a shotgun shell can consist of some number of lead or steel pellets. Some shotgun shells, like buckshot, have a small number of pellets like eight to 15 depending on the specific shell. Each of these buckshot pellets can be up to ⅓ of an inch in diameter. These are typically used for self defense or hunting larger game. Ouch! Other shotgun shells designed for hitting fast moving clay targets or birds and might have hundreds of small pellets in each shell. While more pellets offer a greater chance of hitting the target, they are light in weight and lose energy quickly so they don't travel nearly as far a a rifle of pistol bullet.

So the basic tradeoff with shotguns when compared to rifles is multiple projectiles versus distance. A shotgun is a great tool for hitting targets at close range, like 50 yards or less, while a rifle is great for hitting targets at longer range.

Even though a shotgun fires multiple projectiles, you still have to aim it.

Shotgun shells can contain "shot" or single projectiles called slugs. Left to right: 12-gauge slug, 12-gauge 00 buckshot, 12-gauge 7 ½ shot and a .410 shotshell with 7 ½ size shot.

Speaking of Aiming, We Aim to Confuse!

Shotguns and shotgun ammunition was designed with one primary objective — to completely confuse the uninitiated!

Here's why.

Like other guns, shotguns come in different sizes, where the size really refers to the diameter of the barrel. While handguns and rifles use caliber to indicate their relative size, shotguns have their own system. The inventor of the shotgun naming convention must have been that kid who always raised their hand first in elementary school. You see, most shotguns are measured and named by gauge. Not a gauge. Just gauge. You've probably heard of 12-gauge or 20-gauge shotguns. But there are more. While not as common, there are also 10-gauge, 16-gauge and 28-gauge shotguns. If you live in the UK, shotguns sizes are referred to "bore" and not gauge.

So here you are thinking, "no big deal, shotguns have gauges." And you might assume that the bigger the gauge, the bigger the shotgun. But you'd be wrong. Because it's backwards. Shotguns with smaller gauge numbers actually have larger diameter barrels. So a 12-gauge shotgun is bigger than a 28-gauge shotgun. Why you ask? Well, it's kind of interesting really.

Gauge in this context is a measure of weight. More specifically, it refers to the weight of a lead sphere, measured in fractions of a pound, that will fit into a given diameter barrel. So if a shotgun has a barrel diameter just big enough to fit a 1/12th of a pound lead sphere, then it's a 12 gauge. So a smaller diameter barrel, like a 28-gauge will fit a lighter weight lead sphere in the barrel, or in that case pellets that weigh 1/28th of a pound. Got it?

So now that gauges make complete sense, let's talk about a popular shotgun for beginners and experts — the 410. No worries, it's a 410 gauge right? Nope. It's a .410 caliber. This one is measured more like rifles and pistols where the name refers to the diameter of the barrel in fractions of an inch. 41/100ths of an inch in this case. By the way, it works out to be a 67 gauge shotgun; although no one ever calls it that.

Aren't you glad you asked?

Types of Shotguns

Like handguns and rifles, shotguns have different types of actions.

Break-Action shotguns most commonly refer to double barrel shotguns. Barrels may be mounted side by side or over and under each other. Of course, break-action shotguns are available in single and even three barrel configurations.

Pump-Action shotguns use a sliding mechanism, operated with the non-firing support hand, to load a new shell into the chamber and eject fired shells. Each shot requires operation of the slide. Hollywood loves pump-action shotguns as the heroes and villains look especially studly when racking their pump-action shotguns as they enter action scenes.

Semi-Automatic Action shotguns use the power of gas or inertia from a fired shell to eject a spent shell and load a new one into the chamber. It's a nifty idea to use some of the energy to operate the gun and all else being equal, a semi-automatic shotgun feels like it has less recoil as some of the energy is "soaked up" by the action.

You might also run across some far less common shotgun actions including bolt action and lever action.

Myth: You Don't Need to Aim a Shotgun!

Fact or Fiction? You don't have to aim a shotgun!

A lot of people believe shotguns are great home defense guns, and easy to use, because you don't really have to aim. If you just point one in the general direction of your target and fire, it will clean house so to speak. Right?

Well, in *The Terminator* movie franchise, that's how they work. In the real world, shotguns need a little more skill in order to be effective.

Just because a shotgun fires multiple projectiles, BB's, pellets, buckshot or whatever you want to call them, that doesn't mean that the shot spreads out like a giant cloud of locust intent on devouring a field of ripe Okinawan Purple Sweet Potatoes. It's important to remember that the shot leaves the barrel of your shotgun in a "cloud" exactly the diameter of your barrel. That's a pretty small cloud. To put it in absolute terms, the shot "cloud" leaving a 12-gauge shotgun measures just about ¾ of an inch in diameter.

While it's true that shot projectiles spread out more the farther they travel from the barrel, they typically stay in a pretty tight pattern at realistic distances. That's what that shotgun barrel does after all — keep the shot all together while it launches towards the target. If we're talking self defense, a realistic distance is some fraction of the interior of your house — like across a room or down the hall. At indoor distances, most shotgun patterns are just a few inches in diameter.

The bottom line? You still have to aim a shotgun.

PART II

BUYING A GUN

While gun sales are regulated by the federal government, the process is a lot easier than you might think. Don't be timid about purchasing a gun — it's a natural right, not a privilege granted by the government.

In this section we'll walk you through the process of not only selecting the right gun, but also the process of shopping and buying one legally.

Most people buy their guns from a local gun or big box sporting goods store, so we'll start there. However, buying a gun online is easy — and you just might benefit from a wider selection and lower prices. We'll talk about too. Finally, it's perfectly legal to buy a gun from friends, family, and others with a couple of provisions.

What about gun shows? There's nothing mysterious there, and there's no such thing as a "gun show loophole." Most people selling guns at gun shows are dealers, so the process is exactly like walking into a local store. If you live in the same state as a private seller, that's perfectly legal as well, regardless of whether or not you're at a gun show.

Let's see if we can remove some of the mystery...

SAFE GUN HANDLING

STATISTICALLY, gun-related accidents are quite rare, but even one is too many. Preventing a gun-related incident in your household requires a little knowledge and a lot of diligence.

If you invest in both, you'll never have a problem.

In this section, we'll discuss some common best practices for gun handling. However, there are thousands of guns on the market, each with a slightly different mode of operation. Always refer to the owner's manual for manufacturer recommended safety procedures. If you bought your gun used, no worries. Gun manufacturers almost always post owner's manuals online, so check their website for proper documentation for your specific firearm.

We'll talk about gun handling procedures for different types of handguns, but first, let's review some safety procedures for all guns.

These four cardinal rules of gun safety apply across the board. We'll review them in detail in the Shooting Fundamentals section, but for now, here are the Cliff Notes.

1. Treat all guns as if they are loaded.
2. Keep your finger off the trigger until ready to fire.
3. Never point a gun at anything you're not willing to destroy.

4. Be sure of your target, and what's behind it.

No exceptions!

For some reason, people just love to tinker with guns. Playing, fondling and maybe even caressing. Yes, a quality handgun is a marvel of engineering and can be irresistible to touch. The problem is that there can be life-changing or even life-ending consequences to careless gun handling. That's why it's so important to develop your own rigid and inflexible processes for safe gun handling.

Unless you're in the act of shooting or dry-firing, keep your finger off the trigger!

General Handling Tips

- Every single time you pick up a handgun, verify its loaded or unloaded status. Even if you just saw a salesperson or your range buddy check it, do it again. Any safe gun person won't be the least bit offended that you're double checking. In fact, they'll appreciate your dedication to absolute safety.
- Remember to keep your finger off the trigger while inspecting a gun. That habit alone will get you 12 extra bonus points!
- Keep ammo separate and distant if you're handling a gun. Whether cleaning, practicing dry fire (more on that later) or whatever, you won't want ammunition anywhere near unless you're preparing to shoot.
- Avoid handling guns without reason. The more you handle a gun, the more opportunity there is for something to go wrong. If you don't need to — don't.

- Especially avoid handling loaded guns. If you carry a loaded gun, keep it in its holster when you take it off. The more you can do to minimize handling a loaded gun, the better.

- When you pick up a semi-automatic pistol, always do two things right away. First, while pointing the pistol in a safe direction, open the slide and check to make sure there are no cartridges loaded in the magazine. Second, and even more importantly, check the chamber to make sure there is not a cartridge in there. On a related note, whenever you remove a magazine from a semi-automatic pistol, remember to check the chamber too. Removing the source of new cartridges doesn't guarantee that there's not already one in the chamber!

When checking a semi-automatic pistol, verify that both the magazine and the chamber are empty.

- Last, remember that a gun is ALWAYS loaded. If you treat it as loaded even after you've opened it to verify that it's empty, you'll be even more careful and won't do unsafe things like pointing at objects or people you really don't want to shoot.

Due to the wide variety of action types, we can't cover every type of procedure here. But we don't need to. Gun manufacturers do an excellent job of documenting safe practices for loading, unloading and checking their specific models. Read that manual! If you don't read the manual for your new TV, it's no big deal. You might have trouble changing the channel. If you don't read the manual for your handgun, the consequences are much worse.

Modern guns are designed with layers of safety features. For example, most new guns are drop safe, meaning that they can't discharge simply from falling onto the floor. In fact, you're far more likely to inadvertently press the trigger trying to catch a dropped gun. So, as hard and unnatural as it seems, if you lose control of your gun, let it fall. Any potential scratches or dings are far better than possible consequences of a negligent discharge.

The bottom line is that a carelessly handled gun can cause you to do life-altering and very permanent damage.

Be careful out there folks!

HOW TO PICK THE RIGHT GUN

Many newer gun stores have a range too. You can work with an instructor or even "rent" different guns to try before you buy.

IF YOU'RE BUYING a new handgun, it's good to approach the process with just a bit of strategic planning. The more you can think through some basic decisions, the better the choice you'll make. Not only will you be happier with your purchase, but you also won't experience the dreaded buyer's remorse. Here are a few tips to get you started.

Try before you buy!

The very best way to buy your first gun is to hire an instructor for an hour or so and ask him or her to bring a few different guns. Any experienced instructor will have a variety of handguns in their personal stash. If they don't, look for a new instructor! Have them show you some of the basic shooting skills with a couple of different gun types and brands. You'll quickly see what you like — and what you don't. As an added bonus, having a qualified instructor supervise your testing and evaluation will ensure that you are handling each type of gun correctly so you can make a fair appraisal. Many a fine gun has been tossed aside when a new shooter didn't know how to handle it properly or the nuances of how to make it run just right.

What defines the "right" gun for you?

For defensive purposes, the "right" gun is the most powerful one with which you can hit your target quickly and consistently. If that's a .22 caliber pistol, then so be it. A .22 pistol that gives you the confidence that you'll hit your intended target is more effective than a .45 caliber with which you miss. Make no mistake; bigger and more powerful is always better for self-defense, right up to the point where you can still safely and properly handle the gun and engage your target with confidence. But many new shooters need time, training and experience to reach their "full-power" potential. Start with what you can control and move up from there over time.

Bigger is actually better.

There is an assumed myth that large guns are too much for newer shooters to handle. First, let's define two types of "large." The first type is large size — as in length, height, width, and weight. The second type of "large" refers to caliber or power. For the first type of "large" bigger is actually better. Here's why.

Remember that guy Newton? Not Wayne Newton, the older,

English one. He determined that every action has an equal and opposite reaction. So let's consider an example. If you fire, say, a 9mm bullet from a one-ounce pocket wonder gun, the force generated by that 9mm bullet going 1,200 feet per second forward will be transmitted backward towards your hand and body. Weighing only one-ounce, the gun is probably going to fly at you like a drunken pterodactyl. Now, think about firing that same 9mm bullet from a 20 gajillion metric-ton pistol. The same amount of force is transmitted backward, but you're not going to feel that gun move very much. All this goes to illustrate that while the recoil force of a given cartridge is the same, a larger gun will "soak up" the recoil and the shot will feel less forceful to the shooter.

Here's how it all nets out. A cute and portable 10-ounce pocket pistol chambered in a powerful caliber will kick like an ill-tempered mule. The same cartridge fired from a full-size handgun will be quite comfortable to shoot. Make sense? So, don't choose a smaller caliber just because you tried a pocket cannon that weighs four ounces. Try a larger gun in the same caliber first. As you become more experienced, you can reduce the size and weight of the gun you carry with your chosen caliber as you learn how to make recoil work for you.

Choose your own gun!

Ladies, we're generally speaking to you here. Husbands or boyfriends are not allowed to choose your gun for you! It's important for you to choose your own. The very best way to do this is to invest a few dollars into item number one in this list — spending some quality time with an instructor. Preferably, do this without your significant other there.

Try it on for size.

Just like a pair of boots or that cute little cocktail dress, you've got to try it on before you buy. The gun has to feel great in your hand. Even if you are not able to test shoot it, check to make sure that the grip fits your hand comfortably. Can you reach the trigger without stretching or changing your grip? Does your trigger finger rub along the side of the gun when you press the trigger? If so, the grip is too large for you. Find a gun where you can operate the trigger freely without adjusting your grip or touching the side of the gun. Can you operate the controls easily without changing your grip? Can you rack the slide without embarking on a pre-range conditioning program? If the answer is "no" don't rule out that gun just yet. See our tips on racking the slide like a pro to learn the right technique.

Make sure that you can operate the trigger without your index finger rubbling along the frame. If there's space between your finger and the side of the gun, you're good to go.

Carefully consider whether all of the prices are right.

Most consumer product buying decisions don't have life and death consequences. With guns, your life may very well depend on the quality of gun you buy. This is not a place to save a few bucks buying the cheapest gun on the shelf. The good news is that modern gun manufacturing techniques allow gun makers to produce fantastically reliable guns at very reasonable prices. If you stick with a big brand name, it's hard to go wrong these days.

Think about ammunition availability.

We've run across a lot of people who have bought some super-cheap surplus gun for self-defense use. At the deal time, buying a gun that was used in the battle of Stalingrad sounds charming and pocket-book-friendly. However, when it comes time to find self-defense ammunition, things aren't so glamorous. Sure you can get 64-year-old crates of surplus war ammo, but finding modern expanding ammunition that is safe and reliable is about as easy as getting Dianne Feinstein to speak at the NRA Annual Meeting.

Not to mention the fact that modern hollow-point ammunition may not work reliably in that old gun.

HOW TO SURVIVE YOUR FIRST GUN STORE VISIT

NOT TOO LONG AGO, a visit to a local gun store would more than likely involve meeting Clem, Bodean, and Clem's other brother Clem. You might spot them sitting around the counter with a few buddies talking about yuppies who occasionally wander in by accident. The highlight of their day might have been glaring at those "new people" who had not yet earned the right to hang out and spin gun yarns.

Gun stores have come a long way. Many look more like high-end retail stores.

Fortunately, those days are mostly behind us. Many gun stores have gone full-auto retail and implemented 20th-century customer-centric ideas like hiring helpful sales staff, designing functional and attractive showrooms and installing electric lights and running water.

This is a great thing, and we love to see new stores competing with each other to offer even better customer experiences. The quality of buying experience is light years ahead of where it was just ten years ago.

Most cities now have more than one modern gun store, many complete with shooting ranges and large showrooms for guns, accessories and ammunition. Stores like this are particularly helpful for new shooters as you can "rent" different guns at the stores' range to see which one you like — before you buy. And you can't beat the one-stop shopping convenience. You can buy a gun, a holster, safes and gun locks, and cleaning supplies all in one place. Fantastic!

Even still, visiting your first gun store can be an intimidating experience. But so can any new experience where you have limited knowledge. Heck, I got a little stressed out going to Wild Birds Unlimited for the first time. I feared I would be instantly exposed as a bird-watching poseur! No worries, they were very polite to me and no birds were harmed in the process.

We've put together a series of helpful tips to help you not only survive, but enjoy your first visit to a gun store.

Think about your "why"

Before you go, think about why you're looking at guns in the first place. Do you want it for self-defense? Or just recreational shooting? Do you plan on hunting? Or maybe you want to get into competitive shooting. If the store you visit is on the ball, the first question they are going to ask you is what you're going to do with the gun. This will help them steer you towards suitable options. Planning ahead will help a salesperson help you.

Bring a friend

Think about bringing a friend who is knowledgeable about guns. Most gun owners truly enjoy helping others get involved in the shooting sports, and they are always looking for an excuse to visit the gun store. "Honey, I can't work in the yard today, I have to help (your name) go and pick out their first gun!" The presence of a "coach" will not only give you confidence but help you ask the right questions.

Consider the real budget

Think realistically about your budget. And I don't mean just the cost of the gun. If this is your first gun, be prepared to invest in accessories. You'll need a couple of basic tools for cleaning. Do you have children in the house? If so, you'll need some way to lock up the gun. Even if you plan to just use your gun at a range, you'll need some type of hard or soft case to carry it in. You don't want to be walking around waving a loose gun! Gun locks are also easy to obtain. Most new guns come with one, and most gun stores have simple gun locks available for no charge.

The other budget factor to consider is the ongoing cost of shooting. That correlates with the caliber you choose. At the extremes, a .22LR rifle or handgun will cost you less than ten cents per shot. You can find practice 9mm ammo in the $.20 per round ballpark. If you choose an unusual caliber like .357 Sig, that might cost you $.40 per shot. Think about the ammo costs in advance, so you're not surprised down the road.

Don't freak out because the sales associate is wearing a gun

Gun stores have to be security conscious. Like jewelry stores and other cash-heavy businesses, you'll find that security is a little tighter than at your neighborhood Fabric Emporium. You'll probably see cameras and possibly some sturdier than normal doors and windows. No worries, there's a lot of valuable stuff in the building, and store owners have to be careful for their protection and yours. Most of what you'll see is for nighttime security. You don't often hear about gun stores getting robbed during business hours, do you? Can't imagine why that is...

When you go inside, you might see that sales staff members are carrying guns! Yep. Just like the jeweler is most likely wearing some of his or her products, employees of a gun store will likely be wearing some of theirs. Again, no worries! That's what they sell. It's also one of the reasons that you never hear about gun stores getting robbed. Gun store employees aren't necessarily being tactical commandos; they're just practicing what they preach.

Demand professional service

If someone doesn't acknowledge you within a reasonable time of you walking in the door or to the counter, think about moving on to the next store. This has nothing to do with gun stores and everything to do with retail stores in general. You're there to learn first and spend money only if that process is satisfactory, so expect to be treated accordingly. If the staff doesn't bend over backward to help a new shooter learn the ropes, find a different store.

Many newer ranges feature member lounges.

Don't be offended

Like many jewelry stores, you might notice that gun store staff will only pull out one or two guns at a time. This is a simple security measure — just like those used for diamond rings. Unlike jewelry, gun store management is responsible to the federal government for each and every gun that passes through their store. If they lose one, they're not only out the cost of the gun; they are in serious hot water with the Feds. Given that the Bureau of Alcohol, Tobacco, Firearms, and Explosives can revoke their license as easily as a Capitol Hill Lobbyist buys a round of drinks, owners have to be exceptionally careful.

Be safe when inspecting a gun

When a salesperson hands you a gun to look at, you want to demonstrate safe and proper gun-handling procedures. Even though guns in a store are "empty" you always want to treat them as if they are loaded.

An on-the-ball salesperson will hand you the gun in a safe manner, perhaps with the grip first and the gun action open. If they don't and hand you the gun with the muzzle pointed right at your body, you have a choice to make. If you're feeling dramatic, dive for the floor to get out of the line of fire. If you want to make a point in a more subtle fashion, nudge the muzzle away from you while accepting the gun. Perhaps they'll get the hint. In all likelihood, you won't have to worry about this. In a well run gun store, the salesperson will open and inspect the firearm to make sure it's empty before even handing it to you. Then they will present it to you safely with the action open and the butt end first.

When you take the gun, return the safety favor. Make sure the muzzle never points at the salesperson or anyone else. The floor and ceiling are acceptable options depending on the store.

As soon as you get the gun, you want to open and inspect it. Look at the magazine and the chamber. Stick your finger in there to make sure it's empty. You may feel silly since the salesperson just did this, but you'll be safe. Remember, our goal is to enjoy this shopping experience with minimal gunfire. Besides, if the person helping you knows what they're doing, they won't be offended in the least that you're re-checking what they just did. They'll appreciate your attention to safety and good gun-handling practice.

When you're holding a gun to test it for size and feel, keep your trigger finger straight alongside the frame of the gun. With most modern handguns, it's perfectly fine to pull the trigger to test it out. When I say perfectly fine, I mean that it won't harm the gun. If you want to test the trigger to see how it feels, first ask the salesperson if it's OK if you "dry fire" the gun. If they say yes, double check the "empty" status of the gun and point it at a safe backstop as you do so.

Dry Fire

Dry firing simply means going through the motions of shooting the gun, but with no ammunition. You're cocking the gun (if necessary) and pulling the trigger. This is typically done for practice or maybe to test out the action on a gun. By dry firing, you can get a really good feel for the quality of the trigger on a gun as there is none of that distracting flash and bang going on. There are serious safety procedures to consider when dry firing. Rather than repeat them here, we'll refer you to the section later in the book that discusses dry firing in detail.

Confess

If you don't know the first thing about guns and shooting, tell the associate. Be honest. The more the salesperson knows about your specific situation, the better they'll be able to help you. Pride and ego have no place here. You're investing in a piece of equipment that could save your life, so take full advantage of what the salesperson can teach you.

Get a second opinion

Shopping for your gun can be fun, so it's not a chore to get a second opinion. Like any other retail business, you'll encounter some sales folks who talk a convincing game but don't know as much as they should. Take your time, shop around and get advice from multiple stores. After a couple of visits, it will become clear who is steering you in the right direction.

Big box sporting stores like Cabelas, Bass Pro Shops, Academy Sports, Gander Mountain and others are spreading faster than hairballs at a Yeti convention. Like modern gun stores, these mega-stores are likely to carry everything you need. I've also found the selection to be excellent and prices very competitive.

On the other hand, it's hard to beat the value of a long-term relationship with a smaller business. You'll probably pay a bit more, but when you need help down the road, the local business is likely to be there for you. If the price is your primary consideration, then try some big-box retailers.

If you're shopping for a gun, think about who the long-term user will be. Is this gun going to be "yours?" This question may sound a bit strange, but unlike most any other products except maybe Cialis prescriptions, it's a federal felony to purchase a gun on someone else's behalf. This is one of those laws already in place to discourage convicted felons and those not legally allowed to possess guns from simply getting someone else to buy on their behalf. If the gun is going to be for you, great. If it's intended for someone else, bring them along so they can do the paperwork in their own name.

If gun stores are new to you, just remember that they are a retail business like any other. The good ones will not only help you learn the basics; they'll be thrilled that you're there. As a new shooter, you'll need not only a gun but all the surrounding accessories like ammunition, cleaning supplies, targets, and more. The smart stores will make you feel welcome, so if you're not getting that loving feeling, move on.

MAKING A GUN PURCHASE

BUYING and selling guns is just about the most regulated activity there is.

The first concept to understand is that we are subjects of an overlord known as "the Federal Government." They make an infinite number of laws and rules whenever they're not busy campaigning, having scandalous affairs and cheating on their taxes. One of the laws that the Federal Government flatulated is the Gun Control Act of 1968. This law was established, not coincidentally in 1968, to codify how gun sales would work from that point forward For purposes of this topic, we'll limit our discussion to two components of the act:

1. Prohibition of direct sale or mail order of firearms across state lines.
2. Mandating the federal licensing of companies and individuals engaged in the business of selling firearms. Licensed organizations and individuals are commonly referred to as FFLs.

GUN WORDS EXPLAINED

Federal Firearms License (FFL)

What's an FFL? That stands for Federal Firearms License. It's a piece of paper that documents genuine, bonafide proof from the US Government that says your firearms dealer is legal. FFLs can legally sell firearms to qualified individuals in face-to-face transactions. In other words, FFLs are legally allowed to buy and sell guns for business purposes.

So, to summarize, there are two important takeaways from the Gun Control Act of 1968. No one, except FFLs, can sell firearms across state lines. You can't buy from an FFL in another state directly, nor can you buy from a friend or family member in another state without FFL involvement.

There's a more recent law that also impacts how you legally buy a gun from a retailer. That would be the Brady Handgun Violence Prevention Act. Initially, this law mandated background checks for all firearm purchases from retailers. In 1998, the National Instant Criminal Background Check (NICS) system was implemented. With that in place, a gun sale from your local store looks like this.

Here's the Form 4473 you have to fill out for a background check when buying a gun from a retailer.

1. After selecting the gun you want, you fill out an ATF (Bureau of Alcohol, Tobacco, Firearms, and Explosives) form 4473 Firearm Transaction Record. This form asks for detailed contact information and leads you through a

series of questions where you validate your legal authorization to purchase a gun. For example, if you're a convicted felon, there's a space to indicate that on the form. If you meet any of the disqualifying criteria, you won't be able to buy a gun.

2. The dealer takes this form and calls into the NICS system run by the FBI. They'll do an instant background check to make sure you don't have any disqualifying incidents on your record.

3. In the vast majority of cases, if you come back clean, the NICS people will authorize your dealer to proceed with the sale. In some cases, there's either a denial or a delay. If you have a criminal record, you'll get a denial. There are plenty of cases where a false denial comes back, usually as a result of your identity being confused with someone else. In other cases, you might get a delay where the NICS folks have to dig deeper. Your dealer will let you know if there are any issues. In some states, if you have a concealed carry license, you still fill out the form 4473, but the dealer does not have to call it into the NICS system because you've already been background checked out the wazoo as a concealed carry permit holder.

While it sounds complicated, the process is fast and easy provided you haven't gotten into trouble with the law.

BUYING GUNS ONLINE!

YOU CAN BUY all sorts of things online. The Jack LaLanne Power Juicer, Vince Shlomi's Slap-Chop food processor, the Ninja Cooking System and even a Brazilian Butt Lift kit, not that I need a butt-lift kit.

You can even buy guns online. While not quite as easy as ordering the Proactiv Skin Care System, it's probably more fun even if it won't improve your complexion.

How would you buy a gun online you ask? Well, let's start with a short quiz to check your internet armament shopping knowledge. After you answer, we'll take a closer look at why one answer is right, and the others are incorrect.

Which of the following is an effective way to purchase a gun online?

A. eBay: Search for "illegal assault weapons of doom" or something roughly equivalent. When you find a suitable match, bid like Congress investing in Solar Power companies until you win.

B. Craig's List: Check the listings in your area, hit the ATM for a wad of cash, and drive to your next encounter with destiny. Preferably alone and at night.

C. Answer one of those emails requesting your assistance in moving $20 million into the United States. Perhaps the former Prime Minister of Mozambique wants to sell some guns before fleeing the country?

D. Visit a reputable online seller like Gallery Of Guns, Cabelas, or Brownells and make a purchase online.

If you answered A, eBay, you made a valiant, common-sense effort, but unfortunately, it won't work. For starters, it's illegal. If you read the previous section, then you know that every time you buy a gun from a retailer, you need to complete that Form 4473 and a background check. That applies to online purchases too. Hold that thought for a second; we'll come back to it.

The other problem with the eBay plan is that eBay has all sorts of restrictions on items they deem inappropriate. Guns and parts fall into that category, but the list changes from time to time. It seems every other day they ban some other class of products, so before buying or selling anything firearm-related there check the current policies. But remember, you can't buy or sell a complete gun there anyway.

Many of the newer online retailers look like any other internet shopping site. The benefit is huge selection and prices are usually great. On the other hand, you won't be able to check out the gun before you buy.

If you answered B, Craig's List, then you thrive on reckless danger. If a guy is selling a gun on Craig's List and wants to meet you downtown at 2 am because that's when he gets off work, you may want to reconsider your gun purchasing plan.

You might be safer booking a trip to Ciudad Juárez, Mexico and telling a bartender you work for the Policia Federal. Ask him where you can buy a new Uzi gun and some meth. I'm sure he'll be plenty helpful!

If you answered C, International Financier Connections, well, why not? The odds of legally getting a gun that way are just as solid as the odds of getting your 25% commission for your assistance with moving the former Prime Minister's fortune.

If you guessed D, you're on the right track. You can buy guns online! However, it's not like you hear on the news. Let's explore the process in more detail.

Here are the steps to legally buying a gun online!

1. Go to a reputable website and search for the gun you want. We're kind of partial to GalleryofGuns.com and Brownells.com as they have a huge selection and pre-existing relationships with thousands of local dealers for delivery. There are plenty of others, just check reviews first. If the website you're buying from has a domain name that ends in .ru, .kp, or scam.com, you may want to keep looking.

2. Once you find the gun you want, at the price you want, buy it! Most online sites will require full payment up front, but others like GalleryOfGuns.com operate through a collaborative effort with local dealers. In those cases, the online seller will take a deposit, and you'll pay the balance when you pick up the gun. Hold that thought for a hot second.

3. Now that you have bought and paid for your gun, it will not be shipped to you!

4. The online seller will ask you to have a local (meaning in your state of residence) FFL dealer send them a copy of

their FFL certificate. Your dealer's FFL certificate will have their local address, so the selling dealer knows where to ship the gun. This is getting more and more automated with each passing day, so some online sites allow you to specify the FFL on the purchase page and the paperwork is automatic in the background. There's a list of all FFLs maintained by the Feds so dealers can check each other that way.

5. At this point, the seller has your money, but they also have a document from your local dealer, certified by important government officials, that gives them an authorized shipping location. Now they can legally ship your gun to the local FFL dealer you specified.

6. Next, the selling dealer ships your gun to your local (again, in-state) dealer. You still have not laid eyes on the gun you bought and paid for, but be patient, that time is coming soon.

7. When your dealer receives your gun, they call you to come pick it up.

8. When you go to pick up your gun, you will have to fill out the Form 4473 we discussed in the previous section. The Form 4473 requires you (the buyer) to fill out personal details like your name, birth date, citizenship information, favorite pastel color and whether or not you like waffles. The Form 4473 also has lots of true/false questions that inquire about your eligibility to buy a gun. Are you currently in jail? Have you been convicted of illegal things? Do you intend to buy this gun for yourself or to send to Syrian rebels? In short, you'll answer a dozen or so questions. Be absolutely truthful here as incorrectly filling out a Form 4473 is a big-time federal crime.

9. Your FFL dealer will call the FBI to complete the NICS background check we outlined in the previous chapter. Your FFL dealer will most likely sound bored and

uninterested while speaking to the FBI as both parties do this about a thousand times a day. The FBI will check their records to make sure you are eligible to buy a gun. If you've been a good boy or girl, the background check will come back positive in a minute or so, and the FBI will tell your FFL dealer to proceed with the sale.

10. Your FFL dealer will charge you some fee, usually $25 to $35 for their trouble. After all, they need to send the seller their FFL, receive the shipment, process the paperwork, do a background check on you and store the records of the transaction forever. It's a big pain in the butt for your local dealer so don't complain too much about the transfer fee. Call your congress critter instead and ask them to repeal silly laws.

11. Take your new gun home!

Exceptions...

The above scenario applies to gun sales that go across state lines. If you see a gun advertised on the internet in your home state, you can certainly contact the seller and make arrangements to see and buy the gun. This is America after all, and private sales between two individuals are perfectly legal. State laws change frequently, and some are mandating background checks for private sales, so check for the latest information in your state before buying from an individual.

The Bottom Line

So, for all the political hoopla about getting guns online, background checks and the underground arms trade, buying and selling guns is still a highly regulated process.

While it takes a few words to describe the process, it's actually pretty simple, and the selling dealers are generally really good about leading you through the process.

I love shopping at local gun stores and shows. I often buy guns, accessories, and supplies locally. But sometimes, that certain something you want is only available online. Or maybe you found a used gun on an auction site that you want to buy. Go ahead! While highly regulated, just like buying locally, purchasing online is safe, reliable and easy.

FAMILY, FRIENDS AND NEIGHBORS

Fine Print

I'm not a lawyer, and I don't play one on TV. While the intent of this section is to provide some guidance on how you can legally buy and sell guns in today's political climate, the laws are changing as fast as Kardashians have babies on TV. Use this as a starting point, but be sure to check the current laws and regulations in your country, state, county, city, neighborhood, block, and kitchen.

WE'RE GOING to keep this section short and sweet due to the rapidly changing legal landscape at the time of this writing. With that said, much to Senator Dianne Feinstein's dismay, it's perfectly legal for individuals to buy and sell firearms in the United States.

There are a couple of provisions to consider.

- Personal transactions require buyer and seller to be in the same state. If the transaction crosses state lines, even if the transfer is between family members, then you need to involve FFL dealers. Refer to the buying guns online chapter for details of this process. Of course, the transaction also assumes that both parties are following their respective state laws.

- The buyer and seller need to be eligible to possess firearms. So, for example, if one party is a convicted felon, the entire transaction is illegal.
- Some states are in various stages of implementing background check requirements for private sales, so check your local regulations first!

The Bureau of Alcohol, Tobacco, Firearms, and Explosives has national jurisdiction over these types of transactions, and you can always check their website for current information.

http://www.atf.gov/content/firearms-frequently-asked-questions-unlicensed-persons#gca-unlicensed-transfer

"A person may sell a firearm to an unlicensed resident of his State if he does not know or have reasonable cause to believe the person is prohibited from receiving or possessing firearms under Federal law. A person may loan or rent a firearm to a resident of any State for temporary use for lawful sporting purposes if he does not know or have reasonable cause to believe the person is prohibited from receiving or possessing firearms under Federal law. A person may sell or transfer a firearm to a licensee in any State. However, a firearm other than a curio or relic may not be transferred interstate to a licensed collector."

Bureau of Alcohol, Tobacco, Firearms, and Explosives

PART III

SHOOTING FUNDAMENTALS

Shooting is a skill. Like any other, doing it well requires two things: training and practice. The training part is where you learn the correct techniques. The practice stage is repeating those learned techniques until you've mastered them.

We're going to talk about some basic shooting tips to get you started. However, this book can never take the place of professional face-t-face instruction. So run, don't walk, and find a shooting class in your area. Or invest in some 1:1 time with a qualified instructor. Nothing can take the place of a pro right there with you on the range. The store where you bought your gun should be able to help you get lined up with a good instructor. So use this book as basic, starter knowledge. Don't let this book, or any other, take the place of personal instruction.

One more thing. We can't cover safe, operating instructions for every single pistol on the market in this book. So always read your owners manual carefully. It will show you exactly how to handle your gun safely.

RULES OF GUN SAFETY

BUYING A GUN IS A MAJOR RESPONSIBILITY — one that requires that you put absolute safety first and foremost in your plans. As you'll see, safety rules are often redundant — you have to break more than one for something to go wrong. Learn these rules. Make your friends and family learn them. Make sure every new shooter you take to the range understands these rules.

Rule 1: A gun is always loaded!

RULE ONE
The gun is always loaded. Or is it punk?
myguncuture.com

Yes. Always. Like Lindsay Lohan and the questions on 60 Minutes. Even when it's not.

Every year we hear about people who are accidentally shot with 'unloaded' guns.

"I thought it was unloaded!"

"I'm sure I unloaded it last time I put it away!"

"It wasn't loaded before!"

"Maybe I was loaded the last time I unloaded it!"

Of course, a gun is not "technically" always loaded. But the intent of Rule 1 is to treat a gun as if it is. If you treat a gun like it's loaded, you tend to change your behavior regarding how you handle it.

- You won't check out the sights by aiming it at someone.
- You won't pull the trigger, unless you're actually ready to fire the gun at a safe target. More on that in a minute.
- And certainly, you won't do anything else careless with it.

Rule 1 is first on the priority list, because it's Rule 1, but also because it covers a lot of safety ground. Treating a gun like it is loaded and ready to fire has a fantastic ripple effect that makes everyone around safer.

So take it seriously. Pretend that a gun is loaded every single time you look at it or touch it. Pretty soon you'll start believing that it is actually loaded. Even when you look, and verify that it's not, you'll want to look again to make sure. This is a good thing. Never ignore a gut feeling to check the status of a gun just one more time to be sure.

I like to have some fun with this when teaching new shooters the safety rules. Not for fun's sake alone, but to drive home the point. Immediately after telling them Rule 1, the gun is always loaded, I pick up a gun, point it in a safe direction, and open gun's action to show them. It's empty of course, but I don't tell them that. I ask them if the gun is loaded. It's even better when both kids and adults are present in this new shooter orientation. Almost without fail, the kids look at me with an odd puzzled look for a second, then respond "Yes! It IS loaded!" Kids are much better students than adults. They love getting this trick question right! Adults tend to score about 50% on this pop quiz. About half of them cautiously inspect the gun, then tell me that the gun appears to be unloaded. We all have a quick laugh when I tell them, "WRONG! It's ALWAYS loaded!" Then they get it.

So be creative when talking about the rules of gun safety with others. You can have fun teaching people to be safe — and just maybe they'll tend to remember a little better!

Rule 2: Keep your finger off the trigger until ready to fire!

RULE TWO
Keep your booger hook off the bang switch.

Modern guns are extremely safe mechanical devices. While you should never rely on any mechanical device for safety — as anything can fail — it's really, really unlikely that a modern gun will fire without someone or something pressing its trigger. Most guns can be dropped or even thrown with no risk of firing. Others require one — or more — safety devices to be deactivated before a trigger pull will even allow the gun to fire. So more than likely, when you hear a story about a "gun just going off" you can assume that someone, somehow, moved that trigger.

All of these are reasons why Rule 2 is so important. It's nearly impossible for a modern gun to fire without someone or something pressing its trigger. If your finger is not on the trigger, it sure is hard to inadvertently press it!

Rule 2 might be the hardest habit for new shooters to cement in their memory. The trigger is a hook after all. That makes it a perfect finger rest. You have opposable digits that are designed to grasp things. All of your available fingers prefer to move together in the same direction, so when the middle, ring and pinky finger close around a gun grip, the index finger wants to close also. The natural and instinctive motion when picking up a gun is to grasp it with your finger on the trigger.

It's a massive temptation and a terribly unsafe habit that needs to be broken through practice and repetition. Scientists say that it takes 1,000 to 2,000 repetitions of an action to firmly establish an automatic reflex in your brain. The same concept applies to learning how to keep your finger off the trigger.

It's fairly easy to train someone not to put their finger on the trigger when they pick up a gun. A few reminders will usually solve that problem. But there is far more to developing safe trigger discipline. It has to become an ingrained reflex no matter what the scenario. Immediately after your last shot, does that finger come off the trigger? When changing magazines, does your finger come off the trigger? Does your finger come off between the last shot and setting the gun back down on the table or putting it back in a holster? What if you have to move during the middle of shooting? Will your finger automatically come off the trigger? What about if you are interrupted or startled while shooting? Will your brain still remember to tell your finger to back off?

So training yourself, or others, to keep the finger off the trigger until ready to fire is a chore. Reminding someone over and over to get their finger off the trigger can ruffle some feathers. But you can make the training process respectful, un-intimidating and even fun. When taking new shooters to the range, I tell them (with a smile of course) that I'm going to have to remind them frequently to remove their trigger finger. With some discussion beforehand, no one gets defensive when you have to nudge them at the range. You can also have your family and friends train you. Just ask them to watch you shoot while focusing on your trigger finger.

Rule 3: Never point a gun at anything you're not willing to destroy!

RULE THREE
Don't point your gun at anything
you're not willing to destroy.

Besides, pistol whipping can be a great alternative. Nah, just kidding!

We like to keep things simple around here. You'll hear lots of terminology variations that describe rule 3.

"Never cover anything you're not willing to destroy!"

"Don't muzzle anything you're not prepared to shoot!"

"Always keep the gun pointed in a safe direction!"

"Never let the muzzle cover anything you're not willing to destroy!"

"Point the muzzle only at non-targets!"

While there are lots of ways to describe Rule 3, we like the direct approach. After all, not everyone understands the terminology of "covering." To a novice shooter, "covering" or "muzzling" could have meanings more related to group hugs than where a gun is pointed.

Muzzle

A muzzle is the fiery end of a gun. It's where the bullet comes out. It's the hole in the end that you never, ever, ever want to be looking at.

If you want to get technical, it's the front opening of a gun barrel. Since we're talking about muzzles, it's a good time to mention the other end of the barrel. Located in the back, it is referred to as the breech. Breech, back. Muzzle, front. Simple right?

The key word in Rule 3 is never. According to the Random House Dictionary, the word "never" has two definition components.

1. Not ever or at no time.
2. And to no extent or degree.

The "to no extent or degree" part is actually the most important when considered with Rule 3.

It's fairly obvious that should not stand around and keep a gun pointed at someone or something that should not be shot. It's far less obvious to think about "pointing" as the act of allowing the muzzle to point at someone or something for the briefest instant. It's still considered "pointing" if that muzzle simply moves across something you don't intend to shoot.

I like to tell shooters to envision the muzzle of a gun as a mega-powered, laser-beam, lightsaber of doom with no off button. This destructive beam continues in a straight line from the gun muzzle to infinity — and beyond. This beam waves around wherever the gun muzzle points — all the time. So if the muzzle "points" at something, even for a microsecond, that certain something is destroyed.

The muzzle beam of destruction is activated whenever you touch a gun. It doesn't matter if it's in a gun store, a show, at the range, in your home, or in a gun holster. When you touch it, the beam turns on, and you have to watch every single movement for every single instant. As you move the gun around, what does that beam cross? Or, if you set a gun on the table to do something to it, where is it pointing? I see this scenario at the range all the time. If there is a malfunction, people will set the gun down to work on it, not realizing it's pointed at the shooter next to them.

It may sound obvious as you read this, but Rule 3 includes your own body and extremities — not just those of others. Consider where the muzzle points as you pick up a gun, inspect it, put it away, draw it from a holster or whatever. Be especially cautious of muzzling your arm or leg as they tend to move around and have a great probability of being in the wrong place at the wrong time!

Rule 4: Be sure of your target and what's behind it!

RULE FOUR
Always be sure of your target. And what's behind it.
And behind that. And behind that. And behind that...

Bullets tend to go through things. That's one of the reasons they are so good at being bullets.

So, the key part of Rule 4 is the "what's behind it" part. There are two reasons that you need to consider what's behind the target carefully.

First, your bullet may go right through the target and continue out the back, still traveling at high velocity. If it's still moving after passing through the first target, it's still dangerous.

Second, unlike James Bond and The Lone Ranger, it's possible for us mortals to miss the primary target once in a while. And if you miss, there is a zero percent chance that your target will stop your bullet.

Rule 4 uses the words "be sure" for a very good reason. Unless you are absolutely positive about what's behind your target, don't shoot. Being "pretty sure" isn't good enough when it comes to gun safety. If your view is obscured, don't shoot. Be positive.

STAND LIKE YOU MEAN BUSINESS

WHILE THE MOVIE *Weekend at Bernie's* qualified as a cult flick and spawned its own cool dance moves, it really doesn't play well at the range. That's because dancing tends to throw off your aim and make nearby shooters run for cover.

"Doing the Bernie" refers to leaning backward from the waist, so your shoulders are behind your belt line. Your head also leans back, like you're trying to stop a nosebleed.

The "Bernie" might be ever-so-slightly exaggerated here, but almost everyone does it until corrected.

Why do most of us do this the first time we shoot a handgun? That's simple: survival instinct. There's about to be a grand mal noise generated by a contained "explosion" right in front of our face, that's why. What sane person would want their mug even closer to the forthcoming conflagration?

Here's the problem. This tendency to lean back away from the gun has no practical value. There is little chance that your handgun will suddenly turn around and start chasing you, so the position really provides no tactical advantage.

There are a couple of negative consequences to the Bernie lean. If you're already leaning backward, you've given a big advantage to that recoil force that's about be applied in your direction. The bigger the gun, the more likely you are to be pushed off balance. Follow up shots are also more difficult as you have not provided a stable platform from which to control the handgun. Even if it doesn't push you back, the muzzle will tend to climb with each shot because you're not using your body mass and big muscles to hold it down.

Speaking of stable platforms, semi-automatic pistols rely on the shooter providing a stable "backstop" against which the gun can recoil. The sequence of ejection, re-cocking, and loading a new cartridge into the chamber simply will not work reliably unless you apply enough forward pressure.

There are a couple of major "styles" of handgun shooting stances, and each has numerous minor variations.

The Weaver Stance

Place your support side foot forward of your shooting side foot. Put your dominant arm straight out. Use your support side hand to pull back on the gun, keeping the elbow bent, to create some isometric tension.

The Isosceles Stance

Keep both feet roughly parallel to the target, shoulder width apart. Now shove both arms forward to form a triangle. That's where the "isosceles" part of Isosceles Stance comes from. Clever huh?

So which of these is right for you if you're going to ban the Bernie from your shooting? It doesn't make a darn bit of difference because you can obtain a proper shooting stance with either of those methods–or some other.

In fact, we're doing to suggest a third stance for your first outing. When you get comfortable with this one, you can experiment with the nuances of Weaver and Isosceles techniques. Ready? Here it is.

Point the Fiery End Down Range and Shoot

There's just one thing to worry about to master this variation, and it's pretty simple. Get your weight forward. Here's how you do that.

Here, the shoulders are well forward of our shooter's belt buckle.

- Place your feet about shoulder-width apart.
- If you like to put your weak side foot a little forward, great, do that.
- If you prefer to keep your feet side by side, great, do that.
- See, isn't this easy so far?
- Flex your knees a bit. That makes the next step easier and gives you a better shock-absorbing platform. It also facilitates movement which can be a big help in a defensive situation.
- Here's the important part. Bend a little forward at the waist. You'll know that you're bending enough at the waist if your collarbone is in front of your belt buckle. If you're not wearing a belt, pretend you are.
- Roll your shoulders inward and down just a touch. That'll help control recoil even more.
- If you want to jump to advanced steps, feel free to assume the Weaver, Isosceles, or Iron Lotus position. It doesn't

really matter as long as your belt buckle is behind your collarbone. You can also envision resting a penny on your collarbone and letting it fall to the ground. If it doesn't hit any other body parts, then you've got it right.

- Since your shoulders are usually connected to your collarbone, they'll be in an aggressive forward position. This allows your mass and big muscles to control any movement of your gun.

That's it!

You see, when it comes to killing Bernie (yet again), most of the battle is getting your body weight forward. The nuances of arms and feet positions are secondary to that.

You'll be amazed at how little your handgun recoils when you get your weight forward of your belt. You'll make that gun your bit... never mind. Let's just say you will be controlling your handgun–not the other way around.

You never see Chuck Norris leaning away from those nameless henchmen, do you?

GET A GRIP

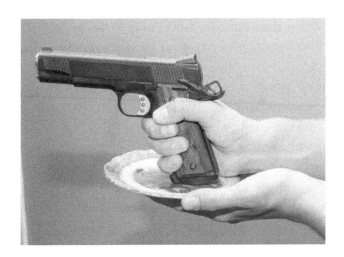

Believe it or not, the most common grip technique error
is about as effective as this.

FRIENDS DON'T LET friends enjoy tea while shooting. Save it for the
post-range-outing ice cream social.

If you read gun blogs or watch videos, you might hear someone
mention a teacup grip. Some call it a cup and saucer grip. Just to be

clear, this is not a compliment or indicator of social refinement. It's an observation of poor shooting form.

The cup and saucer grip refers to a handgun grip style where your support hand acts more like a tea set saucer than a support. The butt of your handgun rests on top of your open support hand palm.

This grip seems perfectly logical but actually hurts your shooting performance.

Let's face it, if you're having tea with Prince Harry, you've got a teacup in one hand and a saucer in the other. The cup holds the tea, so what purpose does the saucer underneath serve? Obviously, it drives up the stock price for Royal Doulton China and adds complexity to the job description of footmen. Other than that, the saucer only serves to catch things that spill. It's a waste of a perfectly good hand that could be used to eat scones.

If you're going to use two hands to shoot a handgun, you might as well get some benefit out of the support hand. Rather than cupping it under the base of the grip like a teacup saucer, how about snugging it right alongside the grip so your support hand fingers can reach around the front? If you're simply resting your dominant hand and gun on top of

Would this style help your golf score?

a wimpy-looking hand-saucer, you're not getting any benefit from the support hand, are you?

You'll be amazed at how little your feisty little pistol or revolver jumps when you use a proper grip. Lack of recoil control is a malady that affects millions of Americans. Only you can help by using a proper grip.

Building a solid grip

With your primary shooting hand, open your thumb and index finger.

Starting your grip as high as possible if the first step.

Push the web of your hand as high as it will comfortably go on the handgun grip, making sure that the barrel of the gun lines up with the bones in your forearm.

This is a solid one-handed grip and also the foundation of a good two-handed grip.

Wrap your fingers around the front of the grip, making sure to keep your index finger out of the trigger.

Do you see some free space on the inside grip panel of your handgun? Good, that's where the bottom part of your support hand palm is going to go. Smack it on there and don't worry if there's not enough room to get your whole palm on the inside grip panel. There won't be, and that's OK.

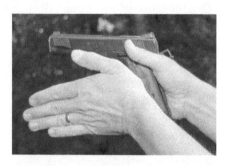

Focus on putting your support hand palm on the grip itself. It won't fit but that's OK.

Now wrap your support hand fingers around the front of your dominant hand fingers. Your support hand fingers should be high–to the point of pressing against the bottom of the trigger guard.

The final product!

You'll know you've got it right if both of your thumbs are somewhere near parallel to each other and touching.

Next time you shoot, notice how much less your muzzle jumps. Your support hand can do wonders to help control recoil when you actually put it to work! Plus, a proper handgun grip looks really cool, so you'll impress your friends at the range. And those forward-facing thumbs? They naturally help you aim. Things tend to go where you point.

FIND YOUR NATURAL POINT OF AIM

If you see something like this when doing this next drill, you might want to keep working on finding your natural point of aim.

WATER TENDS TO RUN DOWNHILL.

Asparagus tends to find its way from kids' plates to the dog under the table.

And Hollywood actors just have to share their political views as if we care.

The point is, all things tend to gravitate towards their natural state.

If there was a way to let your body do more of the work of getting and staying on target, wouldn't you want to take advantage of that? Of course you would!

That's where natural point of aim comes into play. When shooting rifles, handguns, or shotguns, using "natural point of aim" simply means assuming the stance and position where your body naturally wants to point the gun. Perhaps the easiest way to illustrate natural point of aim is to look at unnatural point of aim.

Unnatural point of aim refers to any position where you have to "force" or "muscle" the sights of the gun onto the target. The most extreme example of unnatural point of aim would be standing with your back facing the intended target. Think about all the effort it would take to get your sights on target. Less dramatic examples include assuming any shooting position that requires you to move your arms, shoulders, waist, or hands to "force" the gun into alignment with the target.

If you have to expend any effort at all to "force" your gun to the target, you are creating fatigue in your muscles, eyes, and brain. The second you relax one or more of those, your sights will come off target.

It's one of those "oh, duh" things when you think about it. Shooting from a naturally relaxed and comfortable position will help you shoot more accurately, more consistently, and with better shot-to-shot performance. You'll also get the sights on target quicker if your body is already somewhat aligned when you look for that front sight.

How to find your natural point of aim

The best place to work on finding your natural point of aim is at the shooting range, mainly because it allows you to see your results as you practice. It's also safer because you're already in a place where you can point your gun safely at a target and backstop.

- First, ensure your firearm is on safe and unloaded.
- Next, assume your normal shooting stance with your gun pointed at the intended target.
- Make sure your sights are lined up at a very specific point on the target.
- Close your eyes and take a couple of deep breaths. Think about all those who have passed before us. Do NOT try to force your gun to stay on target — that's cheating. Remember what Miss Ninnymuggins used to say back in fifth grade: you're only hurting yourself!
- Now open your eyes. What do you see? Are your sights still lined up on the target?
- If your sights are now lined up to one side or the other of your desired aiming point, that's an easy fix. Just have the range officer move the target a bit to the side! But seriously, you can do a scaled-down version of the Ickey Shuffle to get your sights back on target. If you don't know what the Ickey Shuffle is, just Google "Best Football End Zone Dances Ever" and you'll get it. Simply put, shuffle your feet to realign your whole body, so your sights line up on target.
- If you find your sights pointed a bit high after opening your eyes, try moving your shooting hand side foot forward just a tad. That can help lower your sights a bit. The opposite works if your aim point is low–move that same foot back just a touch.
- Now, just to make sure you've really found your natural point of aim, briefly close your eyes again. When you open them are you still on target?
- Repeat this exercise until your body position is just right.

Do this exercise repeatedly to make sure your stance is naturally consistent and aligned with your target. Soon, you won't have to close your eyes and dance anymore. You'll find that when you assume a shooting position, your body will find its natural point of aim.

Obviously this isn't something you will do in a tactical or self-defense shooting situation. "Hang on a sec! I need to find my natural point of aim!" The whole idea is to do this at the practice range to build a habit. After a few repetitions, you'll find that you naturally assume a stance that's correct relative to the target.

FOCUS ON YOUR FRONT SIGHT

Here's what you want to see. Notice how the front sight is in sharp focus?

UNLESS YOU HAVE SUPERNATURAL VISION, you're going to notice a bit of a dilemma when you go to shoot your first target.

Your eyes can only truly focus on one thing, at one distance, at one time. In handgun shooting, there are objects at three different distances that you need to worry about:

1. Rear sights
2. Front sight
3. Target

When you line up to shoot, there's a chance that all three of these may appear to be in focus to you. That's because the human brain is an awesome thing. It's processing all three and switching back and forth to create the appearance of simultaneous focus. Or something may look blurry. People see things differently.

However, as a shooter, you'll need to learn to focus on just one of these objects, and that will be the front sight. It's OK if the target is a bit blurry — your brain figures it out, and you can see it well enough to get a hit. It's the same with the rear sights. They are an aid to getting on target, but it's the front sight that's most important.

Front sight focus gets tricky when you're dealing with moving targets or high-stress situations. Your brain naturally wants to zero in on the target. But if you're not focused on the front sight, you'll stand a much greater chance of missing.

So when you dry-fire practice (discussed later in the book) focus on that front sight. Like finding your natural point of aim, it's a habit you want to build, so you don't have to think about it.

One more thought on that front sight. Like a golf or baseball swing, you want to follow through. Following through on your shot simply means keeping your eyes on the front sight until after the shot has left the gun. If your front sight stays on target before, during and after the shot, it's impossible to miss the target. So for each successful shot, you really see two pictures — one before and another after.

PRESS (NOT PULL) THE TRIGGER

THE NUMBER one cause of misses is poor trigger press technique. By listening to shooters at the range, you might assume that a lot of guns shoot low. Or high. Or a bit to the left. Or especially a bit to the lower left. In reality, it's almost always the shooter, not the gun, causing shots to go high, low, left or right.

What's the last thing to happen before the bullet leaves the barrel? That's right, pressing the trigger. Notice we say "press" and not "pull." Pulling the trigger implies a rougher and more aggressive motion.

Here's the root of the trigger press issue. Most handguns require from 3 ½ to 12 pounds of pressure to operate the trigger. On the other hand, most handguns weigh from ½ to three pounds. So when you apply 5 ½ pounds of pressure to the trigger of a Glock 17 that weighs just over two pounds loaded, what tends to happen? Right, the gun wants to move!

Since handguns don't weigh much, the shooter has to figure out how to apply those pounds of pressure to the trigger without moving the gun — at all.

That's where "press" comes into play.

The fastest way to improve your shooting accuracy is to learn how to smoothly press the trigger without moving the gun. You also need to learn how to press your trigger finger independent of the rest of your hand. That's because the rest of your hand is holding the gun!

You'll hear shooters talk about "jerking" the trigger. If you look up "jerk" on Dictionary.com, you'll find a reference to a "spasmodic muscular movement." Being spasmodic is generally not conducive to accurate shooting!

There's no magic secret other than focus and practice. While at the range, tune everything else out except making a smooth, motionless trigger press. Don't worry about accuracy yet. When you master a smooth trigger press, you'll soon see that all your shots tend to hit right near each other. You'll have a nice grouping of holes in the target. Once you reach that point, it's easy to place that group where you want.

Hold this thought. Later in the book, we'll talk about drills you can do at home to master a perfect trigger press.

DON'T BE ALL THUMBS

THE WRONG THUMB position may cause you to bleed all over the shooting range. We don't recommend it.

I can share this new-shooter tip from a vantage point of, um, let's call it "personal experience."

Remember Ghostbusters? And how it's really bad to cross the streams of the Proton Pack particle accelerators? Well, there's a similar rule of thumb (pun fully intended) for shooting semi-automatic pistols. Don't cross your thumbs as in the picture below. Sooner or later, that thing called a slide is going zoom backward at Warp 17 and slice the dickens out of the webby, sensitive skin between your thumb and your index finger.

Slide

The slide is the portion of a semi-automatic pistol that sits on top of the gun frame and houses the barrel. When the gun fires, the slide moves backward very, very rapidly to pull the empty cartridge case out of the chamber, eject it, and load a new one from the magazine. It's got very sharp edges!

If you want to splatter copious amounts of blood around the range, feel free, but once is enough for me. Every single time I go to the range, I see new shooters crossing their thumbs while shooting a semi-automatic pistol. It's a mini-tragedy waiting to happen!

Don't ever shoot a semi-automatic pistol like this. You'll bleed.

Fortunately, there's an easy way to avoid bleeding all over your range. Don't cross the streams. Point both thumbs forward and keep them on the weak hand side of your handgun. Your hand, and your local Doc-in-a-Box, will thank you.

Revolvers present an exception. Since a revolver has no slide or other parts the move backward, you don't have to worry about getting cut. In fact, many revolver shooters prefer to cross their thumbs. If you shoot a single-action revolver, that support hand thumb may be used to cock the hammer between shots.

Bottom line? Be aware of your grip and that of your range buddies. Because bleeding all over the range is embarrassing.

RACK THE SLIDE LIKE A BOSS

HERE'S a stumper that derails many shooters: racking the slide.

With new guns and especially small, compact guns with strong springs, racking the slide can be a challenge. We constantly hear of new shooters turning down certain guns because they can't rack the slide.

Rack

To cycle the slide of a semi-automatic gun. Pulling the slide back draws a cartridge out of the chamber and ejects it to the side through the ejection port in the slide. Allowing the slide to snap back to its original position from spring pressure will strip a fresh cartridge from the magazine (if present) and load it into the chamber. The racking process also cocks the hammer or striker of the pistol, preparing it to fire.

In addition to preparing a pistol to fire, the action of

racking the slide can be used to complete the process of unloading a pistol after the magazine is removed. Racking the slide is also used to clear jams or malfunctions.

On the range, or in a competition, a command to rack the slide may be used in a couple of different circumstances. When a semi-automatic gun is first loaded, the slide must be racked to load a cartridge into the chamber, so the gun is prepared to fire. Second, a range officer may issue a "rack the slide" command when shooting is finished to verify that your gun is empty.

Let us assure you, with very few exceptions, people are in fact stronger than the slide springs. Successfully racking the slide on a semi-automatic handgun is a matter of technique.

The idea is to use natural leverage and larger muscles rather than relying on the small and weak ones in fingers and thumbs. Without instruction, most folks will hold the gun with their firing hand and pinch the back of the slide with their support hand thumb and index finger to pull back the side. While the strong hand is perfectly capable of keeping the frame still against the

This method works, it's just harder as you're relying on the smaller and weaker muscles of your fingers.

spring pressure of the slide, those thumb and finger muscles are not exactly ideal for the job. You've got much larger arm and body muscles right nearby doing nothing, so why not use them? If you're having difficulty racking the slide of your pistol, try following these steps.

First, take a firing grip with your strong hand, making sure that your FINGER IS OFF THE TRIGGER.

Bring it close to your body as shown in the photo.

Next, flatten your support hand and turn it, so that your palm is facing the ground.

Instead of pinching the slide with thumb and fingers, we're going to use the whole hand.

Extend your support hand thumb and jab it right into your sternum. Ouch!

Move your whole flat support hand over the back half of the slide of your gun.

Close it so that your palm is on one side of the slide and fingers on the other. Now you're grasping that slide with your larger hand and arm muscles instead of thumb and finger mini-muscles. Squeeze!

Keeping your support arm in the same place, push the bottom half (frame) of the gun forward like you're going to jab the target with the muzzle.

Notice how, instead of pulling the slide back, I'm pushing the gun forward using stronger shoulder muscles.

See what we did there? Rather than pulling the slide backward, we're tricking you into pushing the whole gun forward.

When you have pushed the gun as far forward as the slide will allow it to go, quickly release the slide with your support hand. Let the springs snap the slide closed. Don't ever try to ease the slide back with your hand. Pistols are designed to work properly when the springs do their job with gusto. If you "help" the slide to close slowly and gently, you're just asking for a malfunction.

A word of caution!

Be careful that you don't do the side slide swipe. The Side Slide Swipe happens when a shooter tries to rack the slide of a semi-automatic pistol while disregarding the direction of the muzzle. Standing at the range, facing the target, the natural motion to rack a slide is (from a right-handed point of view) to point the gun to the left, grasp the slide with your left hand, and rack. The only problem with this method is that your gun is pointed directly at all the shooters to the left of you.

It actually takes a bit of effort and concentration to rotate your body so that the gun is pointed downrange while racking the slide.

DRY FIRE PRACTICE AT HOME

LET'S start off this chapter with a money-back guarantee. If you practice dry firing for a few minutes every day, your shooting skills will improve by 312%. Or maybe 31%. Or 119.3%. But they will improve — a lot. You can bank on that.

Remember that it takes more force to move the trigger of a handgun than the overall weight of it, so it's imperative to learn how to press the trigger without moving the gun. This takes repetition. You can certainly work on this skill at the range with live ammunition. The challenge is that the noise, blast, and recoil all contribute to a very big distraction that makes it more difficult to focus on a perfect trigger press. Working on your trigger technique without all the noise and commotion allows you to perfect the skill. Oh, and it costs nothing so you can practice all you want for free.

I like to think that dry fire practice and flossing your teeth are similar things. Neither activity is fun or sexy, but both make a huge difference over time. So if you want to have teeth like Tom Cruise or Julia Roberts, then floss. If you want to shoot like a pro, then commit to dry firing on a regular basis.

Wait a tic, you may ask, what is dry firing? Dry firing simply means practicing pressing the trigger of your gun without using or firing any ammunition. As a result, you can do it nearly anywhere as long as you carefully and faithfully follow safety procedures that we'll cover here.

Let's talk about how to do it, without harming yourself, your family or your new sofa.

Before we get into the steps, keep in mind that the most important consideration for dry fire practice is safety. You have to develop your own method that insures that you will never, ever, ever have bullets anywhere near your gun when you dry fire. This is because you will be pulling the trigger on your real firearm. The four cardinal rules of gun safety still apply. You'll treat the gun like it's loaded. You'll keep your finger off the trigger until you're ready to fire. You won't point your gun at anything you're not willing to destroy. And you'll be sure of your target, and what's behind it. We're going to follow all of these rules because if all the stars align in just the wrong way, even for a second, and a live round finds its way into your gun, you won't hurt anything except your pride and maybe an ottoman.

Before you start your dry fire practice session

The first step is to remove all ammunition from your gun. Remove it all from your revolver's cylinder or the magazine in your semi-automatic. If you have a semi-automatic pistol, clear the round from the chamber. Stick your finger in there to make sure the chamber is empty. Now, look at the chamber and the magazine well and make sure you see nothing but air. Then do that again.

As for those bullets you just removed from your gun, take them into another room and set them somewhere where you can see them. Now count them. Are there as many there as were in your gun? Next, take any full spare magazines you have and place those next to the bullets in the other room.

The result of all this ammo relocation is that you have taken every round of live ammunition from your gun out of the room where you will be dry-firing.

I like to set up the ammo I removed from my pistol like this near the target so I can see it each time I press the trigger.

While all this may sound excessive, just trust me and do it. Life has far too many distractions and interruptions to be anything less than fanatically safe. If all of your ammo is in a different room, preferably where you can see it from your dry fire practice area, there is simply not a chance that you will absent-mindedly fire a live cartridge.

I faithfully do all of the steps outlined above, but with a slight twist. You'll notice I recommended to place the live rounds in another room where you can see them. I like to put my ammo near my dry fire target. I do this so that every time I pull the trigger on my gun while I am dry fire practicing, I am looking at the cartridges that were in my gun. If I can see the ammo when I pull the trigger, then it can't very well be in my gun, can it? It's just a way that I build in some extra insurance to be positive that my pistol is empty each time I press the trigger.

If you want to get fancy, you can line up the cartridges from the magazine right next to each other. Then I take the cartridge from the chamber and place that an inch or so away from the others. So I have a visual cue of the seven rounds that fit in the magazine of my 1911 pistol, plus the round that was in the chamber. In a sense, I'm looking at a representation of the full capacity of my gun — the rounds in the magazine and the extra that was in the chamber.

How to practice dry firing

Now that we've covered the safety aspects of dry fire practice, what do you do? Let's start simple and add practice exercises.

Basic dry firing simply allows you to practice pressing the trigger on your gun without all that distracting flash and bang. All kidding aside, it's a way to train your eyes, body and trigger finger to press the trigger smoothly, without moving the sights off target. The real benefit is that you can do all this without that instinctive flinch when the gun normally goes bang. By conditioning yourself to a smooth trigger press, without a flinch reaction, you'll eventually find that you do the same with a real gun when it does go bang.

Snap caps are inert cartridges for practice. They're handy for protecting the firing pin and working on drills like reloading and malfunction clearance.

After you've completed the safety procedures outlined above, just follow these steps according to what type of gun you have.

But first a note about .22 handguns!

If you shoot a .22 pistol, you're better off not dry firing that gun. Most .22's do not react well to dry firing due to how the firing pin is placed. The repeated dry firing of most .22 guns will cause damage to the firing mechanism. Most centerfire handguns are perfectly safe to dry fire. Always check your owners manual to see what the manufac-turer recommends.

- Select your target. Make sure that it's in front of a safe backstop that is capable of stopping a bullet. Even though you're following safety procedures, it's important to build in levels of extra insurance.
- Get a comfortable stance.
- Find your natural point of aim by aiming at the target, then closing your eyes. When you open your eyes, are the sights still on target? If not, shift your stance and body position accordingly.
- Here's a great place to pause and remember to focus on your front sight only. Remember, your eyes physically cannot have the rear sight, front sight, and target all in sharp focus at the same time, so you have to pick one. Pick the front sight. The rear sight and the target should both be a little blurry.
- Now, slowly press the trigger as smoothly as possible. The goal is to complete the full trigger press until the gun's action releases — without moving the sights off target at all.
- As the hammer (external, internal or striker) releases, see where the sights are aimed. That's where your shot would have hit had you been firing a live cartridge. Think of this last step as follow through. Dry fire sessions are a great opportunity to train your eyes to see the sight alignment just after the gun "fires." Eventually, you'll know where your shot hit without looking at the target. You'll be "calling your shot."

After your first shot, things will vary a bit depending on the type of gun you have, so let's take a quick look at the steps for each major handgun type.

Revolver (Double Action)

Revolvers are the easiest dry fire gun. After you complete the first dry fire "shot" you don't have to do anything to prepare the gun for the next shot. Simply get your body, grip and sight alignment back in place, aim at your target, and pull the trigger again.

Whether or not your revolver has a hammer, always practice it in double action mode. That is, pull the trigger without first cocking the hammer. That's how you would want to use the revolver in a defensive application anyway, so you might as well get used to it in practice.

Semi-Automatic Pistols (Double / Single-Action)

With a double-action pistol, you can configure your dry fire practice depending on what you want to accomplish. Like a double-action revolver, you can always just pull the trigger to simulate a full, double-action firing sequence. However, in real life, after that first double-action trigger pull, your handgun will cock itself, so the second shot only requires a light, single-action

With a double-action pistol like this Beretta PX4, you can just keep pressing the trigger.

trigger press. Since you're dry firing and there is no automatic cycling of the action, you'll have to pull back the hammer manually to prepare the gun for a single-action shot. So it's up to you if you want to simulate a first double-action shot, followed by a series of single-action shots or some other scenario. Do practice double-action shots, immediately followed by single-action shots though. The transition from heavier to lighter trigger takes some getting used to.

Single-Action Pistols and Revolvers

If you shoot a 1911 style handgun or a single-action revolver, dry fire practice is pretty straightforward. You're going to have to cock the hammer manually between each shot. With a single-action revolver, you want to make the hammer cock part of your dry fire sequence as you'll have to do that in real life. With a single-action semi-automatic pistol, you don't want to build a habit of cocking the hammer each time you pull the trigger. Remember, when you shoot live ammunition, the gun will cock itself after each shot, so you don't have to. To help overcome building "bad muscle memory" when dry firing a single-action pistol, I like to fire the first shot, aim at a different target and simulate a trigger pull and repeat that a few times. After a few "shots" I bring the gun back from firing position, cock the hammer and repeat the exercise.

Striker-Fired Pistols

If you shoot a plastic fantastic pistol that's striker-fired, you have to cock the gun after each shot also. To do this with most striker-fired pistols, you have to rack the slide, as there is no hammer. With most pistols, you don't have to do a complete slide rack. You can pull the slide back ¼" or so and the striker mechanism will reset. Experiment with your gun to see how little of a partial slide rack you can get away with. Like the single-action pistol scenario mentioned above, you don't want to build a habit of racking the slide after every shot, so vary your firing sequence accordingly.

Add some complexity!

Hey, now that you've advanced beyond the simple certificate of participation for dry firing, you can add some steps to build your skills.

    1. Draw from your holster! You've got an unloaded gun, in

safe conditions. What better time to practice your draw? Practice drawing your gun, keeping your finger out of the trigger and evaluating potential targets. Mix in some more complex sequences where you draw your gun and dry fire one or more times. Be creative!

2. Practice magazine changes. How about dry firing your gun and pretending that was the last shot in your magazine? Practice dropping that magazine, pulling a new one and reloading your gun. Be extra careful that ALL magazines you use are empty!

3. Practice malfunction drills. When you dry fire, pretend your gun didn't go bang. What do you do? Practice the clearing drill depending on your particular gun. If it's a revolver, pull the trigger again. If it's a semi-automatic pistol, smack the bottom of the magazine to be sure it's seated, rack the slide, then re-evaluate the situation.

Don't rush your dry firing. That's bad form and will help you develop rotten habits. Your brain is an amazing thing that will build muscle memory of your actions regardless of the speed at which you complete them. Focus on completing your dry fire sequence slowly and perfectly every time. If you do that, speed will take care of itself.

You also might consider a dedicated practice pistol like this SIRT from Next Level Training. It can't fire ammo so it's very safe at home.

After you've practiced and developed the skill of not moving your handgun when you press the trigger, balance a dime on top of your front sight before you dry fire. If you can complete a full trigger press without the dime falling off the front sight, you're getting good!

If you want to get serious about practice at home, you might consider investing in a practice pistol. Companies like Next Level Training and LaserLyte make dedicated, non-function practice pistols. These cannot fire any type of ammunition, so they're perfectly safe to use at home. They are also equipped with lasers that indicate where your shot "hit" so you can get immediate feedback on your technique and progress. LaserLyte even makes targets that react to the laser "strike" so your practice sessions can actually be fun and competitive if you talk a family member into joining.

DRAWING FROM A HOLSTER

Even if you don't have any intention of carrying a gun for personal protection, you'll want to buy a proper holster and learn how to use it. If you ever take a training class, and by all means, you should, you'll need a holster for your handgun.

Earlier in the book, we reviewed safe dry fire practice procedures. Before you practice drawing from your holster, be sure to follow all of the safety procedures we discussed. Make sure your gun is completely empty. If you have a semi-automatic pistol, be sure to empty the magazine first and then remove the round that might be in the chamber. Put all the ammunition far away, preferably in another room.

Before we get into the step-by-step components of a safe draw from your holster, consider the following.

- We're going to present the complete sequence as a series of steps. However, once you get the motions down, the process will be one smooth and continuous motion.
- Practicing your holster draws should be a safe "how slow can you go" process. Safety is paramount. If you go for speed, you're more likely to point the muzzle of your gun

at one of your body parts or at someone else nearby. Take your time.

- You'll get faster the slower you practice. Here's why. If you go slow and focus on performing the draw steps exactly the same way each and every time, you'll "burn" the routine into your brain and body. The concept called "muscle memory" is a real thing. How much do you have to think about stepping on the brake pedal of your car? It's the same idea. You've done that motion thousands of times, so it's now fast, efficient, and completely automatic. If you do your holster draw identically and perfectly in practice, the speed will take care of itself.
- There is a never a need to "speed re-holster." Even in real life, whether on the range, at a competition, or after a self-defense encounter, take your time. Depending on the type of handgun you have, you may need to decock it first, and you want to be positive that our finger is out of the trigger area.

The correct steps to draw from a holster

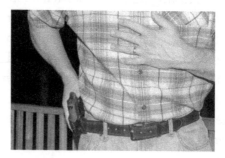

Step 1: Get a grip and get your support hand out of the way.

I. Keeping your firing side elbow close, get a proper firing grip, nice and high, with your shooting hand. Try to grasp the gun grip perfectly on the first try so you don't have to adjust it later. Your elbow will extend backward and close to your side. Also as part of the first step, bring your support hand up and to your chest, placing it right at the base of your sternum. This brings your support hand in close to the body to eliminate the risk of it ending up in front of the muzzle. It also positions your support hand in the perfect place to grip the handgun as you bring it up into a firing position.

1. Draw the gun straight up, keeping your trigger finger along the side of the gun. Only bring it as high as needed to clear the holster. Keep your support hand right where it is on your chest.

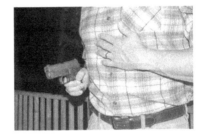

Notice that as soon as you rotate the gun, you can fire because your support hand is out of the way.

2. Rotate the gun forward until it's pointed down range to your target. Rather than thinking of pulling the gun's

3. muzzle up to the target, think in terms of pushing your firing arm elbow down — that will rotate the handgun. At this point, the gun is pointed down range but close to your body. It will also be right near your support hand. If you have to, you can shoot from this position.

4. Bring your support hand to the grip to get a two-handed grip while driving the gun forward. Keep the muzzle at or below the line of the target. What you don't want to do is raise the muzzle above the target so that you have to lower the sight back down when your arms are fully extended. Think of the front sight as rising into view until you have a perfect sight picture.

Once the gun is pointed down range, bring your support hand into position.

If your gun has a safety, be sure you don't disengage it until your gun is pointed down range — never operate the safety while your gun is coming out of the holster!

The last step is to drive the gun towards the target into your normal firing position.

When it's time to reholster your gun, take your time! Be sure the safety is engaged and/or the gun is decocked if applicable. Make sure your finger is out of the trigger. Make sure that all clothing is out of the way. Then, the reholstering procedure is the reverse of the draw.

PRACTICE WITH A PURPOSE

Don't Just Burn Ammo!

Well, on second thought, there's nothing wrong with burning through ammo like Joe Biden burns through hair plugs. Just don't expect to become a better shooter as a result.

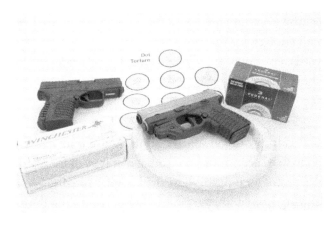

There are plenty of easy ways to structure and measure your practice and progress.

If you want to improve your skills, then you need to embrace boring concepts like goals and structure. But no worries, when it comes to shooting at the range, there are plenty of ways to have fun while improving your skills.

Measuring your progress doesn't have to be complex. You can do that as simply as using a standard round target with scoring rings. Pick a reasonable distance, like yards for starters. Fire ten shots at the target. Add up your scores and write them down with the date. Next time you shoot, do the exact same thing. Pretty soon, you'll have a progression of scores from your range outings so you can track your progress.

Let's talk about a couple of more structured routines that will exercise your skills.

The 45 Drill

Here's one that's simple and fun! It'll also help improve your practical shooting skill — getting shots on target accurately and quickly.

It's called the 45 drill because all you have to remember are four "5"s.

- 5-inch target. We'll cheat a bit and just say paper plate. Because everyone has some laying around and they're small enough for this purpose.
- 5 yards. Position the targets five yards downrange.
- 5 shots. Clear enough?
- 5 seconds.

The goal is to try to get all five shots to hit your five-inch paper plate target in five seconds or less from a distance of five yards.

That's a pretty straightforward drill, right? Ideally, you'll do this drill by drawing from a holster, so the five-second time limit includes your draw. Many ranges don't allow you to draw from a holster, so you can adapt the 45 drill by starting from a low ready position. Just hold the handgun in front of you at about a 45-degree angle aimed toward the ground. At the start of your five seconds, raise the gun, get on target and commence firing. The low ready start method still allows you to practice getting on target.

To accomplish the timing portion of the drill, you can have a friend do it for you using "Start" and "Stop" commands. If you want to get fancy, and have a smartphone, there are free shot timer apps available. These have features that sound a starting beep, then listen for shots. The shot timer will show the number of seconds elapsed between the buzzer and last shot that it heard. You can also set a "par time" which means you designate an interval, like five seconds, and the timer sounds a starting and ending beep.

The Dot Torture Drill

If I had to pick just one practice routine, it would probably be the Dot Torture exercise.

As far as I can tell, this drill was designed by David Blinder at personaldefensetraining.com and modified by Todd Louis Green at www.pistol-training.com. What I like most about this drill is that it exercises a wide variety of handgun skills with one 50-round box of ammunition. The drill has you do slow and accurate fire, rapid single shots from a draw, multiple shots from a draw, single

The Dot Torture drill makes good use of a 50-round box of ammo and works a variety of skills.

hand shots with each hand and even reloads. And the whole 50 round string of fire is scored so you can track your progress over time. Visit www.pistol-training.com to print the targets on standard notebook-size paper. Detailed instructions are on the target itself.

PART IV

LET'S GO SHOOTING!

It's time to go to the range!

Like any new endeavor, the first visit can be fraught with uncertainty and doubt. But never fear, we're going to tell you exactly what to expect, so you can walk in with confidence, know how to be safe, and have some serious fun.

WHAT TO EXPECT AND BRING

What to expect

FORTUNATELY, checking into a shooting range is a lot less stressful than passing through a TSA checkpoint. With that said, shooting range managers need to be careful as the safety of patrons and staff is the number one concern, so there is some process in place.

Many retail shooting ranges may want to take a quick look at what you are bringing into their facility. No, you won't have to go through any TSA pat-downs, but they may ask to look inside your shooting bag. Here's why.

- Indoor shooting ranges have to worry about Rule 4: be sure of your target and what's behind it. If projectiles exit the back of their building, the Jack In The Box customers down the street are going to be really upset. So if you visit an indoor shooting range, you might expect them to check your ammunition to make sure it's not of the steel-core, penetrator type. While great against enemy armor, these types of bullets wreak havoc on shooting range backstops, so many ranges prohibit their use.

- The other thing many shooting ranges will check for is reloaded ammunition. While home-reloaded ammunition can be perfectly safe if you have loaded it yourself following all published safety guidelines, many ranges will not want to accept any related liability. From their point of view, they don't know the source of reloaded ammunition, and it makes little sense for them to take any risk of injury to nearby shooters in the event of a mishap. If your range does not allow reloaded ammunition, it's really not a conspiracy to increase profits — they are simply doing it for the safety of all shooters present.
- Last but not least, your range might want to see what gun you plan to use. As with ammo, different ranges are built to handle different calibers of guns. A short indoor range simply may not have adequate backstops for handguns or rifles that are higher on the power factor scale.

Most ranges will also ask that you bring your guns into the facility unloaded and in some type of case. Many will also want to take a look to verify that your guns are unloaded. At a range, you shouldn't be loading any gun until your on the firing line and ready to shoot.

Your range also might have a waiver, sign-in, and safety briefing process. If it's a retail range facility, you'll almost certainly have to show some identification and fill out a liability release form that says you are responsible for your own safety. Depending on the range, the staff may verbally brief you on their rules and safety procedures, give you a written handout, or sometimes have you

Many ranges now have automated sign-in, liability release, and safety briefings.

watch a safety briefing video before you sign an acknowledgment. If you end up at a shooting range that is not seemingly fanatical about safety procedures, turn around and find another one that is. It's your life after all.

If it's your first time at a range, check-in is the right time to tell the staff that you're new. That will help them help you by offering any extra help on their specific procedures. If you have any questions at all about procedures, never hesitate to ask the range staff. They're there to help and are quite accustomed to helping new shooters get acclimated.

The last thing to expect is nice people! With rare exception, you won't find a nicer crowd of folks than at a shooting range. Don't be a bit surprised if the person next to you asks if you would like to try out their gun or strikes up a conversation about yours.

Renting guns?

The first time I saw a "Guns for Rent!" sign at a Florida tourist destination, I thought the gun nuts had finally gone off the deep end. Of course, I assumed that one could just walk in, rent a gun, and carry it around town during their vacation. Ignorance is bliss...

Now that I know better, I can tell you that gun rentals are a great thing for new shooters. While you can't take them out of the store, you can try them out at the store's own gun range. Paying $10 or $20 to rent a gun is a lot better than dropping $600 on one that you find you don't really like. Most gun ranges have a wide selection of guns to rent. Take advantage of this, preferably before you buy. You can see what works for you before dropping the big bucks.

What to bring

You can buy pretty much anything you might need at a retail shooting range including ammunition, eye and ear protection and gun accessories. Over the years, I've found a few nice things to stuff into my shooting bag. This bag now weighs over 1,200 pounds and can hold a Volkswagen, but that's beside the point.

With that said, here are some things to bring.

Ear Protection

Most every range will have eye and ear protection available for sale or rent. But you re
ally want to avoid that if you can. It's perfectly safe to use, but do you want someone else's ear sweat and eye juice on the stuff you rent? Nah. It's inexpensive, and you'll want to have your own anyway. Let's talk about each for a minute.

OK, it's time to confess. You don't particularly like to wear helmets while riding a bike either because it looks kind of dorky. A helmet just might save your life if you wreck, but most people don't have bike accidents on every ride, so many take the risk and ride without. When it comes to the need for hearing protection at the shooting range, there is no probably. There is only absolutely. As in

You absolutely, positively have to use hearing protection every time you shoot. In-ear and over-the-ear versions are inexpensive.

positively. Every shot you fire without ear protection will permanently damage your hearing. And each additional shot after that will damage it more. You probably won't know it for a while — maybe years — but it will happen.

There are two basic types of ear protection. Inserts that you stuff into your ear canals and external ear muffs that make you look like a Top Gun pilot. Both can be effective if you buy quality. And getting quality ear protection is not all that expensive. You can find perfectly good hearing protection for $20 to $35 in most any gun store or big box sporting goods store.

Generally speaking, the exterior ear muffs will provide a little more protection, but some of the new internal models are getting pretty darn good. If you want to get really fancy, you can get interior or exterior ear protection that electronically monitors sound levels.

Those let low level (safe sounds) like conversation get through to your ear, but block loud (and dangerous) noises like gunshots. You can find exterior earmuffs with electronic filtering for as little as $35. It's really nice to be able to hear your friends and the Range Safety Officer without removing your hearing protection.

Double Up!

If you're shooting at an indoor range, use both interior and exterior hearing protection. Indoor shooting ranges are louder than a full-blown catfight on The View. So, to save your hearing, put some foam plugs in your ears, then add external muffs. You'll be glad you did!

Safety glasses

Eye protection is equally, if not more important. If you shoot, stuff may bounce back at you and hit you in the face. Bullet fragments. Target fragments. Backstop fragments. Irritable forest critters. Or who knows what else? After you've shot for a while, you'll realize just how frequently bits of debris of one kind or another make their

Always use certified, impact-resistant eye protection. You only get one set of eyes!

way back towards your face. Safety glasses also offer protection against burnt or burning powder residue that can eject out of the pistol. Last but not least, in the event of a very rare but possible catastrophic gun or ammunition malfunction, you'll want protection over your eyes. While every shot without eye protection does not result in vision loss, it's only a matter of time before something wrecks one or both of your eyes.

The easiest way to spot a new, and foolish, shooter is to look for those too cool to wear shooting glasses and ear protection. There are thousands of stylish eye and ear protection options out there so you can even look good while sporting your common sense safety gear. Just do it.

Clothing

You wouldn't think you need to dress for the range. But you do. When you or someone near you fires a shot, there is a miniature conflagration inside of the cartridge case. That makes recently fired cartridge cases very, very hot. So if you or someone near you is shooting a semi-automatic pistol or rifle, it will be flinging burning hot brass all over the place.

Here are a few apparel tips to help keep you on the rare, rather than well-done side:

- Hat: A hat the covers the top of your head and that has a bill is a great idea. Even indoors. The brim will help prevent hot brass from falling on your face and worse yet, between your shooting glasses and your eyes.
- Covered shoes: Flip flops and sandals are not the best idea either. Think about how much it hurts when the top of your feet get sunburned. Now think about how burning hot metal would feel there.
- Tight-necked shirt: Guys, avoid loose and open button-downs. Or button them up almost all the way. Ladies, watch the low-cut blouses — cleavage is not a good home for hot brass!

While avoiding getting burned by hot brass is a good idea, there's an even more important reason to dress properly. If you're shooting a loaded gun and hot brass starts to burn the bejeepers out of you, what's the natural reaction? Right. You're going to jump, move, dance, curse and many other things and who knows where that loaded gun will point in the process.

Miscellaneous supplies

- Bandaids and cloth tape: Blisters happen. The more you shoot, the more likely you are to get a blister or two. Some Bandaids and tape for the fingers come in handy.
- Extra eye and ear protection: You are planning on bringing friends right?
- Bug spray for outdoor ranges: Outdoor ranges tend to locate in rustic, woodsy places far from civilization — so you'll be sharing the range with mosquitoes, gnats, and nomadic African bat bugs. Do yourself and your guests a favor and pack some Deep Woods OFF!
- Sunscreen for outdoor ranges: Back to that far from civilization and rustic thing. Some ranges have nice covered shooting areas, and some do not. Plan on some serious sun if you're going to stay a couple of hours.
- A roll of tape: I like to keep a roll of regular masking tape in my shooting bag. It's handy for hanging or repairing targets or covering bullet holes so I can reuse targets.
- Stapler and extra staples: Depending on the target stands at your range, staples might be more effective for hanging paper targets. Don't forget spare staples as the stapler always runs dry 19 seconds after you first use it.
- Extra targets for remote ranges: Indoor ranges will have plenty of targets of different types for sale. Outdoor ranges may not. So keep some in your bag. There are thousands of fun targets that you can print on standard notebook paper available on the internet.

- Water: If you're shooting at a retail range facility, there should be plenty of drinks and snacks. If you're headed to an outdoor or more rustic place, be sure to bring plenty of water. As you get dehydrated, one of the first things you lose is concentration and focus, and that's a bad thing when you're handling guns.

SHOOTING RANGE ETIQUETTE

THE "RULES" of shooting ranges are usually pretty clear. However, as in golf and tennis, there are "rules," and then there is "etiquette." You know, the expected behavior that's not always written down. I'm pretty sure that the United States Tennis Association Officiating Rulebook doesn't include anything about fans painting their chests and starting the wave during the Family Circle Cup, but if you try that, you'll almost certainly be escorted off the premises. That's an example of etiquette.

Obeying the official rules is a must, but it's also important to know range etiquette.

One of the biggest problems with the shooting sports is that there is no be-all, end-all, definitive guide to etiquette. Miss Manners never published a Sooper Dooper Guide to Shooting Etiquette, and I never recall going to the range for any of my charm and finishing school field trips.

Seeing this glaring omission from the shooting community training curriculum, we've taken the liberty of compiling a list. Check out these range etiquette tips, and you'll be safe and looking like a pro shooter, or at least a well-rounded intermediate, in no time flat.

Case Your Guns

No matter where you shoot, you have to get your guns from your home to the range. How you move them up to the range parking lot is your business. How you move them from the car to the shooting table involves your shooting range neighbors. Wandering through the parking lot and into the front door of a secure business waving a few guns around is a great way to have a really bad day. The very best way to do this is to case your guns and move them to all the way to the shooting table fully encased, unloaded and with actions open. This particular etiquette procedure may be a rule at your range too. Regardless, it's not only safe but polite to others.

Check to make sure everyone has ear protection before you start shooting

Yes, a verbal "Range Hot" command should, in theory, ensure that folks have their ear protection in place. Just in case, I like to be considerate and look around to make sure everyone is hearing protected before starting to shoot.

Don't booger hook your trigger unless you're in the act of shooting

As much as we all talk about trigger finger discipline, it's never too much. With perfect trigger finger etiquette, we will all have a perfect safety record. In the context of this list of "polite" actions, think of keeping your trigger finger visibly out of the trigger as a courteous visual cue to your neighbors. If they see you always handling your gun with the trigger finger out, they'll feel safer and more comfortable having you as a range neighbor because they'll know that you take the four rules of gun safety seriously. Sometimes good etiquette is about showing range neighbors that you know what you're doing.

Be visibly cold to your range neighbors

Not in social demeanor, but in behavior. When the range is "cold" for target changes and such, make a physical show of acting cold. By this I mean put your guns on the table. Don't touch them, even if they're unloaded. Because guns are always loaded right? Again, considering the good range neighbor angle, if you aren't touching your guns, folks can easily see that you're not touching your guns. And they feel safe and secure based on your visible behavior. So, looking at it this way, being visibly cold at the range is actually polite.

Bonus tip: If you want to look like a real pro, then don't just put your gun(s) on the table when you hear "Range Cold!" Step away from the shooting table and stay there the whole time the range is cold. This is a "sooper dooper" move that let's nearby shooters know that you are not messing with your gun(s) while the range is cold. It's very considerate, and they will love you for it. Who knows? You might develop your own new relationship while your gun and the table are focused on theirs.

Many ranges allow shooters to reload magazines while the range is cold, as long as they are not messing with their guns.

Lock that sucker open

When not actively shooting, it's a good practice to leave your gun locked open and facing down range. Get ready; you've heard this in other points here — it's a visible signal to your range neighbors that lets them know you're thinking about their safety. And that's always polite.

When not shooting, leave your guns on the table pointed down range and with the actions open.

Don't shoot other people's targets

This means intentionally or unintentionally. Remember Rule 4? Be sure of your target and what's behind it? Pay attention to where your bullets go after they pass through your target—especially at outdoor ranges. If you're shooting at your target from even a slight angle, your shots may be hitting someone else's target further down range. And it's not polite to spoil that killer group they were working on.

Notice how this shooter is positioned right up against the shooting line so her muzzle is forward of it.

Toe the line

Back-row shooters are scary. You know, folks who stand a few feet behind the firing line to shoot, so their muzzle is technically behind you? I don't care if you're Mother Theresa's long-lost Navy SEAL nephew. If your muzzle is behind me, I don't trust you. If you want to be polite to your range neighbors, make sure your muzzle is always in front of the line when shooting. I've yet to see a bullet u-turn.

Look at the bright side, you'll be a little closer to the target and shoot a better group!

No hokey pokey

Turning yourself all around? No, that's not what it's all about at the range. If you just have to turn around to show your friends your .381-inch free-hand group, be sure to put your gun down first. If you turn around and see people around you dropping like former Disney Channel child stars, perhaps you still have a gun in your hand? Feel free to put your handgun forward, and even put your right foot in. You can even do the Hokey Pokey, just don't turn yourself around.

Use the evil eye, when necessary

I know this one doesn't sound like an example of showing good manners to other shooters, but hey, it's for their own good. After a range is called "cold" I always look down the line to make sure no one is playing with their gun. If I spot someone still tinkering when folks are about to walk downrange, I make a slightly dramatic show of stopping in my tracks and staring at them with an innocent, questioning look that says " the range IS cold, right?" I confess this is a bit childish, and maybe passive aggressive, but it sure is effective. For the really clueless ones who don't figure out the body language, a polite reminder to stop playing with their guns when the range is cold is the next step.

Question everything

We shooters have some sort of ego sickness. Meaning we hate to ask for help or clarification. You'd think we were driving or something. Personally, I love it when someone at the range asks me a question.

That means they care about doing things right. So I try to remember the same courtesy. If you're the least bit unsure about procedure or etiquette at the range, feel free to ask. It's polite to be certain before you act. And I've yet to experience anyone giving me an attitude when I asked a safety or procedural question. Have fun, be safe, and ask a question if you're not sure! It's the polite thing to do.

WHAT IF YOUR GUN JAMS?

DEALING With Malfunctions

The loudest sound in the known universe, other than Rosie O'Donnell, is the sound of a "click" when your gun is supposed to fire. We'll refer to that sound as a malfunction. Sometimes there's not even a click and the gun still won't fire. We'll call that a malfunction too.

Fortunately, unless something physically broke on your gun between shots, malfunctions fall into a couple of common categories. Let's take a look at how to deal with them.

If you're at a retail or club shooting range, odds are pretty good that a Range Safety Officer is nearby. In that case, never hesitate to ask for help if you are not confident in what you're doing. Range Safety Officers deal with questions and malfunctions about a thousand times a day and will be able to help you out. Just put your gun down on the counter, muzzle facing down range, and seek assistance. Whatever you do, don't turn around with the gun in your hand and yell "Hey!" That will cause a ruckus for sure.

Revolver Malfunctions

If you shoot a revolver, you have the easiest job of all when it comes to dealing with a malfunction. If you hear a "click" just pull the trigger again. Odds are that you hit a dud cartridge that simply didn't ignite. While rare with quality factory ammunition, it does happen from time to time. If pulling the trigger a second time does not clear up the problem, then it's time to unload your revolver and seek additional help.

If the trigger won't work or the cylinder won't turn, there's no simple and immediate way to rectify the situation. It's possible that a primer has backed out of a cartridge and jammed up the works, a bullet has creeped forward and prevented the cylinder from turning, or maybe there's a mechanical breakage. If you can't open the cylinder, empty the cartridges, and start over, it's time to go to a whole new plan.

Pistol Malfunctions: Failure to Feed / Failure to Eject

A semi-automatic pistol is a nifty invention. The "auto" part of semi-automatic refers to the fact that the gun is designed to automatically eject a spent cartridge casing and load a new one after each shot. Sometimes, things go wrong and the cartridge scheduled for forcible ejection doesn't want to leave. It's the same principle as those relatives from Ohahumpa, Florida who visit at Thanksgiving.

More often than not, a failure to eject is caused by the shooter. Semi-automatic pistols rely on the shooter holding the frame of the gun still during ejection so that the slide and springs have something to work against. If you use a weak grip, the gun moves backward with the slide and that whole bit of fancy recoil mechanism engineering fails. This may cause an empty cartridge case to get stuck in the ejection port. This blocks a new cartridge from being loaded and prevents the slide from closing fully. All this is a long way of saying the gun don't shoot no more.

Sometimes, the failure to eject or feed malfunction is caused by a magazine not being fully inserted into the gun. It may stay in place, but not be fully engaged. As a result, the cartridges in the magazine aren't lined up with the chamber properly and won't feed reliably. Guns aren't pansy toys, they're meant to be operated with vigor. So whenever you insert a new magazine into a semi-automatic pistol, smack it in there like you mean it.

This most common malfunction is one like this, called a stovepipe. The tap, rack, and reassess drill will solve this.

Whatever the cause, to make the gun work again, you have to get rid of the spent cartridge casing and allow the slide to grab a fresh cartridge from the magazine and load it in the chamber.

Here's the solution: It's commonly called the Tap, Rack, Bang drill, but I prefer to call it Tap, Rack, and Reassess. After you "tap" and "rack" it may be appropriate to reassess whether you still want or need to fire before pressing the trigger again. It works like this:

1. Keeping the gun pointed safely down range, enthusiastically smack the bottom of the magazine to make sure it's seated properly in place. That's the "tap" part. Smack is probably a more descriptive term as you don't want to be gentle. The goal is to make sure that the magazine is firmly seated in place.

2. Rotate your pistol a bit to the right so the ejection port is facing towards the ground. Gravity helps here and most pistols have the ejection port on the right side, hence the suggested rotation to the right. Now rack the slide vigorously ONCE. This will (hopefully) clear any spent cartridge casings stuck in the ejection port and load a new round in the chamber. If you rack the slide more than

once, you might be flinging perfectly good ammo from the magazine onto the floor each time you rack.

3. Here's the "bang" part. But we prefer "reassess" — because you may not always want or need to shoot. Do things look normal again? Is the slide fully closed and in battery? "In battery" is one of those fancy gun terms that means "fully-closed" by the way.

If this drill does not solve the problem, it's time to move to the next method of clearing, as you might very well have a double-feed malfunction

Pistol Malfunctions: The Double-Feed

The next most likely malfunction scenario is a beasty one. It's called a double-feed. And it's double trouble because you have to do some rhythmic gymnastics to clear it.

1. The first step assumes you've already done the Tap, Rack, Bang/Reassess drill with no success.

2. Using the slide lock on your pistol, lock the slide to the rear, again keeping the muzzle pointed down range.

A double-feed is more difficult to clear, you'll need to remove the magazine.

3. Remove the magazine. If you do have a double-feed, you're going to have to exert some serious force to remove the magazine. Don't be afraid to use some muscle.

4. Save the magazine. You can tuck it under your shooting hand arm, stuff it in a pocket, or if you have the coordination of a mature spider monkey, hold it between a

couple of fingers. You may need this magazine when the jam is cleared, especially if it's the only one you have!

5. Now rack the slide several times vigorously. There is no magazine in place so you don't have to worry about flinging perfectly good ammo all over. You're trying to clear out anything in the chamber area that might be jamming your gun.
6. Now replace the magazine and smack it into place.
7. Rack the slide one more time to chamber a round.
8. Unless your gun malfunctioned for some other reason, you should be good to go.

If these methods don't clear the problem, then there is more going on that we can't address in the scope of the book. Try getting help from the Range Officer!

Remember, if ever in doubt, ask for help!

PART V

AMMUNITION

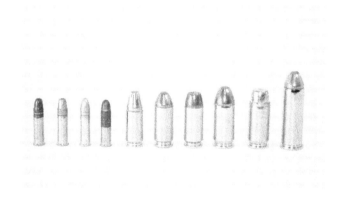

Once you choose a handgun, you're going to need to know a little bit about ammunition. Many gun stores will have literally thousands of boxes of different types of ammunition on the shelves. Let's take the mystery out of it.

AN AMMUNITION PRIMER

HA! AN AMMUNITION 'PRIMER' Get it? If you don't, a primer is a component of a cartridge. So there's kind of a pun thing working there. Still not chuckling? Ok then, let's move on...

Ballistics and ammunition performance is a complete field unto its own, which warrants volumes of research and observations. As this is a Practical Guide, we're going to hit on the high points — the things you need to know if you're going to own a gun. And since this is the Handgun Edition, we'll focus primarily on handgun ammunition. We might venture into rifle and shotgun ammunition where warranted.

But first, let's clear something up. Hollywood does a lousy job of portraying the performance of handguns. Pistol shots cause villains to fly through windows, cars, and buildings to explode and nameless henchmen to surrender by the thousands. In other words, TV and movies show that handguns have serious "knockdown" power. Let's talk about that for just a sec...

An Eternal Myth: Knockdown Power

Lot's of people with advanced social media degrees talk about things like "knockdown" and "stopping" power. While handguns certainly can cause recipients to hit the deck, it's not as a result of a pistol or revolver bullet literally knocking them down.

Remember from the beginning of this book that handguns make holes, and that's about it.

Remember that scene in the movie *Men in Black*? Where Tommy Lee Jones hands newly-minted MIB Agent J (Will Smith) a tiny silver pew-pew-pew pistol? Then when Smith fires it, he's knocked backward 15 feet right onto his toucas? Well, that's exactly what would happen in the real world is handgun ammunition actually had "knockdown" power. If your gun were capable of knocking someone down, you would be on the receiving end of some equally vicious recoil.

Here's why.

If someone tells you about the knockdown power of a given cartridge, immediately run to the nearest library and ask to borrow a copy of Physics For Dummies. In it, you might find mention of a guy named Isaac Newton.

While his brother Wayne was busy developing a fine singing career in Las Vegas, Isaac focused on important issues related to the motion of objects. Among his other accomplishments, he came up with that "equal and opposite reaction" theory. If you want to know his exact wording, translated into English, it's this.

"To every action, there is always opposed an equal reaction: or the mutual actions of two bodies upon each other are always equal, and directed to contrary parts."

What this means that is there is an action (force) going one way, an equal amount of action (force) is coming back the other way. If that bullet you fired as enough force (more on that in a second) to knock someone down, then there's enough force coming back in the opposite direction to knock the shooter down. Just like Agent J in *Men in Black*.

So that's the simple explanation in Newtonian physics terms. Let's put that into more practical perspective. In the guns and shooting world, there are two common measures of "power." I put that word in quotes because I'm taking a surface-level approach to physics.

The first is kinetic energy. Commonly measured in foot-pounds, you can think of the kinetic energy as "destructive power." While not a perfect analogy, I envision kinetic energy as a power drill. It exerts a lot of chaos on boards and such but doesn't impart much actual force on an object. When you drill a hole in a piece of lumber, the wood doesn't go flying across the room. As an example, 9mm ammunition has a kinetic energy measurement of somewhere around 350 to 400 foot-pounds depending on the bullet weight and velocity.

The second common ammo "power" measurement is momentum. This one does represent the ability of the projectile to move an object. If something has lots of momentum, it can knock something else down. That same 9mm projectile might have momentum of about 19 pounds-feet per second.

So how much "oomph" is 19 pounds-feet per second? Well, a baseball hurled by Aroldis Chapman can reach 51 pounds-feet per second and Nolan Ryan on his best day can deliver 52. Both of those are over double the momentum of a 9mm bullet. Lest you think 9mm's are particularly wimpy, a .40 S&W generates about 27 pounds-feet per second, and a .45 ACP creeps up to about 28. So none of them have more physical "knockdown" power than a major league baseball pitch. As a side note, a bowling ball hurled by a pro packs a whopping 422 pounds-feet per second of momentum. I'm thinking that would probably knock one down and leave a serious mark.

So the point here is that barring a million other factors, handgun bullets simply don't have enough energy to knock someone out of their shoes and through a plate glass window.

Yet some (certainly not all) people tend to hit the ground when shot. Why? Well, it could be one or more of a myriad of reasons. Fear is a leading contender. Bodies are naturally disinclined to want to be shot again. Pain certainly has an impact. Sometimes, a structural element like a critical bone is broken, taking away support and causing a tumble. In other cases, a cause might be "electrical" damage. A disruption in the ability of the brain to communicate with muscles can cause all sorts of weird things from collapse to erratic movement.

Don't believe me? Next time you have an opportunity, take a 25-pound bag of sand to the range and prop it up on a stool. Heck, you can even stick something on the front, so the bullet doesn't pass through, thereby delivering all its "oomph" to the sandbag. Guess what'll happen when you shoot it?

Not much.

RIMFIRE AND CENTERFIRE

ALL MODERN AMMUNITION works essentially the same way. Put it in a gun, press the trigger, and it fires.

But seriously, virtually any type of ammunition operates the same way. Cartridges have the following components:

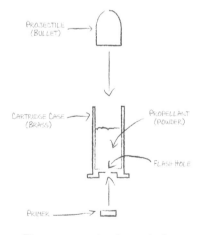

The components of a centerfire cartridge.

- Primer: Inside the base of a cartridge is a compound that's sensitive to impact. It converts the mechanical energy of a firing pin to a chemical reaction. When struck, it literally explodes causing a flame to enter the cartridge and ignite the powder inside. As we'll see, some types of cartridges use a removable cup to hold the primer compound and others have it applied directly to the inside of the cartridge case.

- Cartridge Case: Usually constructed of brass, but sometimes steel, the cartridge case has either a hollow cup for a primer or a hollow base filled with primer compound. It also contains the propellant powder and holds the bullet or projectile in place. Until fired. It's the part left over after a bullet is fired.
- Propellant Powder: Back in the old days, cartridges used black powder which technically explodes. Modern cartridges use a variety of fast-burning (not explosive) propellants which create a large volume of expanding gas really, really fast. The pressure of this expanding gas is what pushes the bullet down the barrel and out the muzzle.
- Projectile or Bullet: This is the thing that actually launches out of the gun.

The only real difference between rimfire and centerfire ammunition is how the primer is placed and where the firing pin strikes.

Here are the four components of a centerfire rifle cartridge: primer, case, propellant, and projectile.

Rimfire Ammunition

Rimfire ammunition has a hollow rim (hence the name rimfire) around the interior base of the cartridge. This hollow base is filled at the factory with priming compound. The firing pin strikes the outside edge of the cartridge, thereby squashing the priming compound underneath the firing pin. As the priming compound gets squished, it bursts into flame and ignites the propellant in the cartridge. This, in turn, makes a whole boatload of rapidly expanding gas, which propels the bullet forward.

.22 Long Rifle rimfire cartridges.

Modern rimfire cartridges include the .22 Long Rifle, .22 Short, .22 Magnum, .17 Mach 2, .17 Hornady Magnum and .17 Winchester Super Magnum. Many others have come and gone, but you're likely to see these on store shelves. As the priming compound is "molded in" to the cartridge case, you can't reload rimfire ammunition as it's hard to get priming compound back into the hollow rim of the case. Besides, after the first firing, there's a dent in the case rim from the firing pin impact.

Centerfire Ammunition

The primary difference between centerfire and rimfire ammunition is the location and method of primer insertion. Centerfire cartridges use a separate primer cup that's about 3/16 of an inch in diameter give or take. These separate primers are inserted into a hollow area at the base of the brass cartridge case. The hollow area just happens to be in the center, hence the name "centerfire." As the primer is a separate component, it can be removed after use and a new one inserted in its place. The new primer cup is already charged with priming compound, so for all practical purposes, the cartridge case is again like new. This allows industrious folks to reload centerfire ammunition.

The cartridge case on the right has the primer removed. The one on the left has been fired — you can see the dimple from the firing pin strike.

When it comes to rifle versus handgun, it makes no difference. There are centerfire rifles and handguns. There are also rimfire rifles and handguns. It's more of a cartridge thing.

Make sense?

PRACTICE AMMUNITION

IT'S important to understand the difference between practice ammunition and self-defense ammunition. You can use self-defense ammunition for practice, although it will put a major dent in your wallet, but you really don't want to use practice ammunition for self-defense.

Practice ammo bullets are normally coated with copper jackets but new approaches like this Syntech from American Eagle use polymer "jackets."

Practice ammunition is designed for... practice. At risk of offending my friends in the ammunition business, practice ammo is designed to:

- Fly forward when fired.
- Go as straight as possible.
- Go bang every time it's struck by a firing pin.
- Be relatively inexpensive to encourage people to practice more.
- Make holes in paper.
- Be safe to the shooter and the gun.

Modern practice ammunition is excellent and exceeds all of these design parameters. It works. It's affordable. It's been proven safe and reliable by millions and millions of rounds fired by shooters like us, law enforcement and military personnel. The only potential problem occurs when people ask it to do what it's not designed to do.

As we'll discuss in the next section, self-defense ammunition is designed to stop threats as quickly as possible. Not kill or wound, but stop. It's also designed to do that while minimizing the risk to others who may be behind the attacker. That's an important distinction. If someone is fighting for their life and fires a lethal round at the attacker that takes 10 minutes to kill that attacker, was it effective? Not really, as the immediate goal is to stop the attack as quickly as possible. A lot of damage can be done by a determined attacker in that 10 minutes. As a contrary example, what if that round never killed the attacker, but somehow discouraged them from continuing to attack? Effective? I would say yes.

Practice ammo is usually constructed using full metal jacket bullets. This simply means that the lead core of the projectile (bullet) is covered by a copper or similar metal to contain the lead and prevent it from gunking up the inside of gun barrels. When FMJ bullets hit something, they just keep going. They might get squashed a bit, or break apart in extreme cases, but generally, they make relatively small holes in things before continuing on their way.

When using this FMJ design in self-defense situations, the tendency to make small holes and keep going presents a problem. Making small holes in a determined attacker doesn't necessarily slow them down. It might or might not depending on the location of the strike and the determination of the aggressor. Worse yet, FMJ bullets tend to go right through relative soft targets and keep on going. So what, or whomever, is behind that attacker is now also potentially in danger.

Strangely enough, studies have shown that FMJ ammunition is actually more lethal to the person being shot than expanding hollow-point ammunition as more shots are required to stop the attack. While not immediately lethal, the after effect of more shots increases lethality.

The net result is that you should always use practice ammunition for practice. Yes, it's dangerous and lethal to the attacker, but may be less effective as a defense tool and more dangerous to bystanders.

Besides, if you're practicing, you'll want to use the most affordable ammunition you can get provided it works safely.

SELF DEFENSE AMMUNITION

SELF-DEFENSE AMMUNITION IS EXPENSIVE STUFF, often priced around the one dollar per shot range. That's because it is specifically engineered and manufactured to do amazing things.

Self-defense ammo isn't cheap, but that's for a very good reason.

Most defensive ammunition is designed to expand when it

encounters a soft target like the human body. This expansion has two primary objectives.

1. It increases the size of the wound and likelihood of stopping an attacker.
2. Keep the bullet in the target thereby delivering all energy to the target while minimizing the risk that the bullet will pass through and potentially impact unintended people or objects.

In addition to these two characteristics, increased wound size, and control of over-penetration, you have to consider adequate penetration. This is where the engineering magic comes into play. The FBI and other law enforcement agencies have done extensive testing to determine just exactly how far a bullet needs to penetrate a target to be effective. Consideration needs to be given to barriers like clothing, jackets, bone, automobile windshields and other obstacles that may stand in the way of a projectile fired at a target. Entire books are written on this topic alone. For now, we'll keep it simple.

Most self-defense ammo uses a hollow-point bullet design that causes the projectile to expand when it hits organic targets.

Your self-defense ammunition needs to provide adequate penetration, reliable expansion, and minimize over-penetration. Piece of cake right? Well, not really. That's why self-defense ammunition costs a dollar per round.

While most modern self-defense ammunition lives up to its marketing claims, there are still variables to consider. For example, the barrel length of your gun. You might have decided on a 9mm semi-automatic pistol as your handgun of choice. But 9mm semi-automatic pistols come in all shapes and sizes. Some have two-inch barrels while others have five-inch barrels. Barrel length is one of the variables that wreaks havoc on ammunition performance because the shorter the barrel, the lower the velocity of the bullet — all else being equal. In our testing, we've found (for handguns) that each single inch of barrel length reduction results in a velocity loss of about 30 feet per second. The velocity difference between the same self-defense cartridge in a two-inch barrel gun and a five-inch barrel gun can be 100 feet per second!

Ammunition design is a careful balancing act between bullet expansion and penetration capability. Manufacturers test performance using ballistic gelatin blocks like this one.

As expansion performance of self-defense ammunition is correlated with velocity, that just might determine whether your bullet expands properly or not.

Since it's unlikely that you're going to test a bunch of bullets with fancy ballistic gelatin setups, stick with the big brand names like Sig Sauer, Speer, Federal, Winchester, Cor-Bon, Double-Tap and Buffalo Bore to name just a few. Some manufacturers like Speer have developed special versions of ammunition for short-barreled guns. For example, they offer standard 9mm cartridges in their Gold Dot line, but they also offer Short Barrel 9mm Gold Dot cartridges. These are specifically engineered to properly expand at lower velocities while still providing adequate penetration.

One final note about self-defense ammunition. There are lots of advertisements for exotic self-defense ammunition that supposedly provides explosive performance of doom and destruction. You might hear claims that a single round can bring down a herd of irritable Wildebeests or level a city block. Don't get sucked into the hype until you are confident and knowledgeable about exactly what you want your ammunition to do for you. Traditional hollow point ammunition is used by virtually every law enforcement officer in the country for a reason. It works, and its performance has been documented for decades. If you ever find yourself in the situation of having to defend your choice of ammunition, wouldn't it be nice to say you simply chose the same ammunition that the local police force uses?

RELOADING AMMUNITION

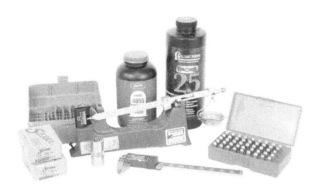

RELOADING ammunition can be a great hobby for men, women and responsible young adults.

I'm one of those guys who enjoys reloading. Yes, I can save some money on a cost per round basis – if I place an hourly value on my time somewhere below the cost of a Wintergreen Tic Tac. The main reason I reload is that I like to tinker. Why experiment with 42 varieties of .357 Sig ammunition? Why shoot lead bullets at 1,000 feet per second out of my 1903 Springfield surplus rifle? Why not?

If you might have an interest in reloading in the future, start saving the brass cartridge casings now. If your range allows you to pick up your brass, you'll want to start saving your centerfire spent cartridges like 9mm, .38 Special, .40 Smith & Wesson, .45 ACP and other similar calibers. .22 Long Rifle is not reloadable as it uses priming compound built into the cartridge rim itself.

While reloading is a science unto itself, we wanted to mention the idea here and point you to a couple of resources. The first place to start is with our book, The Practical Guide to Reloading Ammunition. It'll help you learn the concepts and step-by-step procedures.

PART VI

ACCESSORIES

Lights, lasers and night sights are not just cool, they dramatically improve your ability to safely use your gun in low light conditions. You'll also need a holster, even if you don't intend to use your handgun for concealed carry.

HOLSTERS

AT THIS POINT, you've successfully navigated a gun store and come out alive. It's time to talk about one of the most important accessories you can buy — a quality holster.

Whether or not you plan to carry concealed, you really need a good, solid and safe holster. They're handy (and safe) to use at your range (specific range rules permitting.) You'll almost certainly need one to take any sort of self-defense class. And drawing a gun from a holster is one of those skills you should develop if you're going to own a gun.

Far too many new gun owners purchase a really nice gun but then skimp on the quality of their holster. Seriously?

Whatever you do, don't skimp on your holster. Get a good one like the Galco Combat Master shown here.

You wouldn't drink a Louis Roederer, 1990 Cristal Brut from a red

Solo cup. Unless of course, you're attending a Real Housewives of Yulee, Florida baby shower.

If you've been invited to carry the Dubai First Royale MasterCard, you certainly wouldn't whip it out at the Monte Carlo Van Cleef & Arpels from a velcro wallet.

So why do people think it's no big deal to buy a $9.95 holster from K-Mart for their brand new gun? It's not like it's a life and death investment. Or is it?

A Word on Concealed Carry Holster Selection

Not many choices you make on a routine basis carry life and death consequences. One that just might is the choice of how you're going to carry your handgun. Outside of competition and recreational range time, the situation where your holster absolutely and flawlessly needs to perform is when you are forced to protect yourself.

To understand the ramifications of making the right choice for your unique situation, you have to consider what your holster and carry method must do. At the very highest level, the combination of concealed carry style and holster must keep your gun secure at all times while still allowing you to access your handgun safely, consistently and quickly.

Let's set forth some criteria about what a good holster needs to do. You might consider these three factors as you evaluate different methods.

Gun Security

Carrying a firearm in public is a big responsibility. You are ultimately responsible for anything that happens with your gun. You need to know, without doubt, that your handgun will stay secure throughout your daily activities. Whatever you do, whether it be sitting at a desk, getting in and out of vehicles, or vigorous physical activity, your carry method and holster need to ensure that your gun remains right where it should — on your person.

That's the liability perspective. It goes without saying that your gun needs to be available at the moment you need it most. If it's fallen out during your daily travels or shakes loose during a self-encounter, your firearm, training, and practice are all for naught. It's kind of like training for years to compete in the Olympic Biathlon event only to show up on the big day without your skis.

Trigger Protection

Modern handguns are designed with lots of safety features, but there's still one constant. Guns only fire when the trigger is pulled. It's up to you to prevent that. When you're handing the gun at home for maintenance or at the range, Gun Safety Rule Two applies. Keep your finger off the trigger until you're ready to fire. However, when your gun is concealed, you also need to think about trigger safety.

If you carry your gun in a purse, briefcase, or pack without a holster, it's entirely possible that some other object can work its way into the trigger guard and cause a discharge. This actually happens far too often. Just to be clear, that situation is not an accidental discharge. You created the conditions that allowed something to interfere with the trigger.

There are other common scenarios too. People who carry an unholstered gun in a pocket face the same risk. Car keys or other objects can and have caused negligent discharges leading to serious injury and even death. Carrying a gun in the waistband without a holster is another accident waiting to happen. There have been documented cases of people shooting themselves while frantically reaching into their pants trying to prevent a gun from slipping out of position.

The takeaway is simple. No matter what carry method you choose, make sure that the applicable holster has trigger protection features. Traditional waistband holsters completely cover the trigger. Make sure that nothing can reach the trigger until after you draw your gun.

Accessibility

We've saved accessibility for last because it's the factor that most new concealed carriers take for granted. If you ever need to draw your gun in self-defense, there's no such thing as getting to it "too quickly." You need it, and you need it now. You might need to access your gun while actively fighting off an attacker. You might need to be able to access it from an awkward position, perhaps rolling around on the ground. You might need to access it with just one hand or while running.

If you're considering carry a gun for personal protection, check out our book, The Practical Guide to Gun Holsters for Concealed Carry. It will go into far more depth on carry methods and specific holster options than we can cover here.

NIGHT SIGHTS

NIGHT SIGHTS OUGHT to be required like seat belts, food labels and poop buckets for Clydesdales.

Well, required might be a little extreme, as many guns are purchased for daytime recreational use or other purposes. But if you own a self-defense gun that did not come with night sights, please seriously consider adding them.

In our opinion, the most effective night sights are ones that use tritium inserts. These are tiny crystal tubes filled with radioactive tritium gas. The tritium glows at night and never requires a light source to initiate its glowing. So

These TruGlo TFO tritium sights improve both day and night visibility.

it's not like those star and moon stickers you plaster all over kids room ceilings. Usually, tritium sights will last about seven years before they start to go dim.

You can expect to pay between $100 and $130 for tritium sights for most pistols. There are all sorts on the market for most any modern handgun. We'll list a few of the major manufacturers here.

- Trijicon trijicon.com
- AmeriGlo ameriglo.com
- XS Sight Systems xssights.com
- Meprolight meprolight.com
- TruGlo truglo.com

Depending on your specific gun, you may be able to swap the factory installed sights for night sights yourself, but many pistols really require a special sight pusher tool. The gun store that sells you the sights will almost certainly be able to install them for you.

GUN LIGHTS

HAVING read millions of shooting articles, attended self-defense classes and shot hundreds of different guns over the past 15 years, I thought I knew the importance of weapon-mounted lights.

Then I shot at Zombies in a cave.

Weapon-mounted lights are now small, light, and affordable. It's a great addition to consider for a home-defense handgun.

At the 2012 Shooting Industry Masters event, Surefire, a maker of tactical weapon-mounted and hand-held lights, set up a cave match. We're not talking virtual cave or simulated cave. We're talking the kind of cave you access by finding a hole in the middle of the woods. You then climb down a rotting ladder into that hole, squeeze your slightly-out-of-shape butt through a rocky entrance that's about three feet tall. You then crab crawl for a bit and navigate 20 yards or so of 18-inch wide winding crevasses. At this stage, you can mostly walk. After proceeding another 100 feet or so into the cave you are completely blind. I mean completely. The point of all this cave talk? The shooting environment was dark. Really dark.

The match instructions were simple. Using a Glock equipped with a light and laser, you proceed deeper into the cave and shoot any three-dimensional Zombie targets you encounter. Without getting bitten. While Zombies aren't real, yet, and you're not likely to be clearing any caves with a Glock, the experience was very enlightening. See what I did there?

This Crimson Trace Rail Master Pro adds both a light and laser to any handgun with a rail.

Anyway, the net-net of all this experimentation and numerous other training events in dark and low light conditions is this.

Technology can be cool. Just a few years ago, lights on handguns were limited to the domain of uniformed police officers wearing huge holsters on four-inch wide duty belts. Thanks to technological advances in miniaturization, battery performance, and electronics durability, we now have light and laser combinations perfectly suitable for home or even concealed carry use.

If you consider lights as an addition of capability, then there's no reason not to have them available assuming that there is no undue "cost" in terms of bulk and weight. In low light conditions, a light allows you not only to see but verify, your target before you pull the trigger.

Here's the gotcha. Lights on a handgun are great for shooting in the dark but a terrible solution for looking around. Sure, it's convenient to search using your handgun with a light. You just walk around like a Delta Seal Ranger Ninja and light up everything suspicious. The problem is that this approach violates basic gun safety rules. You never, ever point your gun at anything you're not ready and willing to destroy. Ever. If you're searching with the light on your gun, you're by definition pointing it at things you haven't yet identified.

This is why a light on your gun is an addition to shooting capability, not searching capability. If you decide to put a light on your handgun, that's fine, as long as you keep a separate flashlight right next to it for looking around in the dark. Use the weapon-mounted light for shooting and the flashlight for looking.

LASER SIGHTS

LIKE WEAPON-MOUNTED LIGHTS, laser sights are one of those things you don't fully appreciate until you try them.

These Crimson Trace Master Series Lasergrips add no bulk to this 1911 pistol.

Some instructors will scoff at laser sights because they insist that shooters should learn to use the iron sights on the gun. I couldn't agree more. All shooters should become proficient at shooting with iron sights. Those don't break or run out of battery juice, so you can count on them to work.

What laser sights do is add are new options to shooting the old-fashioned way. They don't replace the basics. Just as headlights on a car add the option of driving at night, laser sights add several new capabilities.

- They provide an excellent low-light sighting option. In dark conditions, the red or green laser dot shows up brilliantly on your target.
- Lasers make a great training aid, especially for dry-fire practice. If you are not executing a perfectly smooth trigger press, you'll see that laser dot bouncing around like hamsters wired on Red Bull.
- Lasers allow you to aim from unusual positions. If you shoot around a corner or obstacle, you might need to aim with the gun not exactly at eye level.
- Lasers also support the natural tendency to focus on the target. Since the bullet strikes where the dot is, you can focus on the target and the dot simultaneously.

So, just as car headlights don't take away your daytime driving skills, lasers don't remove your ability to shoot with regular iron sights.

Crimson Trace (www.crimson-trace.com) offers a complete line of laser grips for nearly all modern handguns. What we like about the Crimson Trace offerings is that most models feature

With many pistols, you can add both a light and laser.

instinctive activation. The laser "switch" is either on the front, back or sides of the gun grip, so when you assume a normal firing grip, the laser is automatically activated. There is no need to remember to turn on another switch or lever manually.

You might also want to take a look at offerings from LaserMax (www.lasermax.com) and Viridian (www.viridiangreenlaser.com.) Both companies make quality integrated laser products too.

Having a laser on your handgun won't make you a better shooter. However, used properly in practice, it can facilitate the process of you becoming a better shooter.

OPTICAL SIGHTS

PUTTING optical or red dot sights on handguns isn't a new thing. Competitors have been doing it for years and with great success. What is new is how they're moving onto mainstream guns like those for recreation, home defense, and even concealed carry. The inevitable march of technology has made them small, amazingly durable, and affordable.

Optical sights are great for plinking guns like this Smith & Wesson Victory.

To be a bit more specific, a red dot sight is generally a holographic approach. The unit projects a red dot (sometimes other patterns) onto a small window that's mounted on top of a revolver or pistol. The shooter looks through the window at the target. Unlike traditional iron sights, there is nothing to line up. Just place the dot on the target and shoot. It's very simple and very fast.

Small red dot sights like this Trijicon RMR mount right on the slides of many semi-automatic pistols.

Advantages

- Aiming with a red dot is simple and intuitive. You don't have to worry about coordinating the rear sight, front sight, and target. Just place the dot where you want to shoot.
- Red dot sights facilitate our natural tendency to focus on the target. Our brains want to do that anyway, so this type of sighting system allows us to follow our instinct so to speak.
- Those with older eyes will likely find that red dots are a

great visual aid. There are no tiny sights on which to focus. That red dot is bright and easy to see for most anyone.

- Red dot sights work equally well in daylight, low-light, and dark conditions.
- Red dot sights are great for first-time shooters. Since sighting is so simple, they can focus on technique rather than lining up iron sights.

Disadvantages

- Optical sights are electronic and like anything else they can break. Modern options are shockingly durable, however, so it's unlikely you'll have any trouble with a quality model. Since the dot is projected, you'll still be able to use an optical sight with a cracked lens.
- Finding the dot takes some practice. It's a different approach if you're accustomed to using iron sights so you'll need to get used to it.
- You have to remember to change the batteries, especially if you rely on a handgun with optical sights for defensive purposes.

If you're considering using optical sights on a recreational hand-gun, there is no downside. They're fun and make it easier to hit small targets at longer ranges. If you're considering getting into competitive shooting, most types of competitions have divisions where optical sight usage is fine. If you want to use optical sights on a home or carry gun, then be sure to dedicate time to practice and training, so their use becomes instinctive. And be sure to change batteries on a regular basis before they run out.

PART VII

GUN CARE AND FEEDING

OK, so maybe gun care and maintenance isn't quite this simple, but it's a lot easier than you might think. By design, guns are amazingly durable tools, and it's pretty hard to damage them inadvertently. However, there are a couple of mortal enemies to your gun, and the primary one is rust. Let's take a quick look at some tips for cleaning and storage that will keep yours running in tip-top shape.

CLEANING YOUR GUN

IF YOU WANT MORE than a simple certificate of participation as a shooter, then you need to think about how you're going to clean your guns. Modern guns are fantastically good at taking abuse from dirt and grime. However, there comes a time when you'll have to clean it.

The first step is taking it apart, or, as gun gurus say, field stripping.

Field Strip

No, field stripping has nothing to do with Woodstock flashbacks.

Field stripping simply refers to taking your gun partially apart to clean it.

Manufacturers design guns so that the major components come

apart easily to make the gun easy to clean and lubricate. If it's hard to put back together after a simple cleaning, then there's a chance it won't work right. And manufacturers certainly don't want to hear about someone's gun not working right when they really, really needed it. So a simple field stripping procedure is in everyone's best interest. Certainly yours!

This Beretta PX4 is field stripped and ready to clean.

We can't cover all field stripping procedures here since every gun is different, so you'll have to refer to your owners manual. Be very careful because many firearms require the trigger to be released as part of the field stripping procedure. Make sure that your gun is completely unloaded, including the chamber, before starting to field strip!

Gun cleaning supplies aren't expensive. You probably already have most of what you need.

First, you're going to need some basic supplies. There are more gun cleaning supplies and magic solvents on the market than Congressional Idol contestants, but don't let that discourage you. It's hard to go too wrong with any gun-specific cleaners and oils. Notice we say gun-specific. What you don't want to do is use a general purpose penetrating oil like WD-40. We love WD-40, and it's wonderful for many things. You may even use it to clean gun parts. Just don't rely on it as a preservative and protectant for post-cleaning use. Guns tend to get really hot, hence the need for special oil and lubricant formulations that are designed to stand up to intense heat. Heck, you can even use motor oil to lubricate guns, so they're not all that picky.

At risk of setting a herd of apoplectic gun treatment vendors on my trail, I do want to highlight the importance of using the good stuff. Yes, motor oil will work, but save that for the apocalypse. I'm not a doctor, nor do I play one on TV, but the word is that burning motor oil fumes are not something you want to inhale on a frequent basis. Instead, use cleaners, lubricants, and protectants that are specifically designed for guns.

One challenge is that there are infinity plus one gun potions on the market. The good news is that most of them are fine.

And they're not all the same. Some are designed specifically for cold conditions. Others are designed to operate dry, so they don't attract fine sand into the guns' actions. Others are designed to clean only and not protect. Some are specifically designed to remove lead residue, others copper residue, and others the plastic residue from shotgun shells. The labels are very clear about this, so read carefully and experiment to your heart's content. You're not very likely to hurt anything. There is one caveat — of course! If your gun has part polymer construction, check to make sure your solvent is safe to use with polymer.

Once you've chosen your cleaner and lubricant — and sometimes they are in the same bottle — you'll need a couple of high tech tools and disposables to clean the gun.

Get yourself a scrap of indoor-outdoor carpet for a cleaning pad. It's cheap as dirt, will not get all slimy with cleaning solutions and oil and does a great job of keeping small parts from rolling off the dining room table. You can find scraps for next to nothing at most home improvement stores. Your spouse will thank you.

One of my favorite budget cleaning tools is an old toothbrush. While rough on teeth, those nylon bristles aren't going to scratch gun metal or even the polymer frames on modern pistols. And they have a nice big handle so you can clean vigorously!

The next thing you'll need is something to clean out the inside of the bore (the barrel.) The traditional solution to this is a cleaning rod with a female threaded end. The end can accept an attachment that allows you to affix cloth patches for removing dirt and cylindrical brushes for removing stubborn residue from the inside of the barrel. You can find these simple cleaning rods in kit form, complete with various size brushes and cloth patches at any gun store.

One of the very portable OTIS Cleaning Kits.

We're going to pause and put in a plug for what I believe to be the best cleaning system on the market. It's called the OTIS Technology System. As the story goes, the founder of OTIS, Doreen Garrett, age 16 at the time, was hunting with her Dad and got hung up on a muddy root. Doreen and her Winchester rifle pitched headlong into mud, clogging up the barrel with swamp goop. In desperation, and trying to salvage the hunt, Doreen tried to use a stick to clear the mud, and the stick promptly broke, clogging up the bore even more. With hunt-less hours in the cabin to reflect on solutions to the problem, Doreen dreamed up the OTIS System. From her experience, the system had to be field-portable. But also, it was designed to clean guns from the back to the front (breech to bore) to minimize risk of damaging the crown of the barrel. The result was design of a stiff, but flexible coated wire with various attachments for cleaning. As the "cleaning rod" was flexible, it could be rolled up into very portable field-ready kits. Now that's American ingenuity!

So if you want to save yourself some trouble, consider getting an OTIS Technology System like the one shown here. It's well worth the money and the kits are designed to accommodate rifles, shotguns, and pistols of various calibers.

I like to start by dragging a solvent-soaked patch through the barrel.

Since your gun is field stripped, you have access to the barrel. Let's clean that first. Using the cleaning rod with a cleaning loop attached, stuff a cloth patch through the loop, apply some cleaner or solvent and push (or pull) it through the barrel. Ideally, do this from the breech to the muzzle as this will pull gunk away from the action and out the muzzle.

Once the solvent has gone to work, brush the crud loose.

Now you can attach a brass wire brush. Push or pull that through in the same direction a bunch of times. This will loosen stubborn stuff in the barrel like powder, lead, and copper residue. The solvent you dragged through in the first step will be working to loosen dirt and mung while you do this. If you are cleaning a revolver, and want to do a bang-up job, repeat these first two steps for the barrel and for each chamber in the cylinder.

Be careful when scrubbing the action not to knock loose small parts and springs.

Last, put your cleaning loop back on the rod and load it with a dry patch. Run that through. If it comes out dirty, put a clean patch on and repeat the process until no more dirt is coming out. Finally, check the instructions on the cleaner or lubricant you chose to see if they recommend leaving a light coat on the inside of the barrel. If you used a pure solvent or cleaner, you will need to finish the process by applying a thin film of lubricant or protectant.

Use lots of fresh patches to remove dirt. See how quickly they get nasty?

Now you get to look for dirt on the rest of the gun. Be careful not to go crazy with that cleaning toothbrush as there are small parts and springs, like slide lock levers, that can get knocked off with vigorous cleaning. Until you learn the intricacies of your particular gun, be slow and methodical. Use a little cleaner, scrub with a brush, then wipe away dirt with a cloth cleaning patch or rag. Always do the wiping with a clean patch or section of rag, so you're removing loose dirt rather than just moving it around.

You probably want to clean your magazines as well. Wipe them down with a dry cloth and make sure you don't get oil inside the magazine. Oil and bullets don't mix all that well! Once in a while, you'll want to take apart your magazines and wipe the inside clean. They tend to accumulate dirt over time. Just refer to your manufacturer instructions.

When you're finished, apply oil sparingly. Your owner's manual will tell you exactly where to put it.

The last step is to apply small amounts of lubricant. Your owners manual will show you the exact spots where this needs to be applied. Unless the manual says otherwise, less is more. The more oil you slather around, the more likely it is to attract dirt, so lubricate sparingly!

Modern guns are engineered to really take a beating, and it's pretty unlikely that you'll do it any harm by cleaning. Relax, read your owners manual, and clean away!

Using all dry-fire precautions, test your gun to be sure you put things back together correctly. Some people like to clean their gun at the range when they are finished shooting. This way, after reassembly, they can fire a couple of test shots to make sure the gun is put back together in working order. That's another benefit of using one of the portable OTIS Technology kits.

STORING YOUR GUN

THERE ARE two major considerations to storing your guns.

First and foremost is safety. Anytime your gun is not on your person; you need to assume complete responsibility for its security. Is it safe from little hands? Is it out of sight from visitors? Is it in a safe condition — meaning locked away? Just be aware that some home, office and car solutions are intended to provide gun security and others are only intended to provide a simple holstering mechanism, so know the difference, and plan accordingly.

The second consideration is care. Are you storing your gun in such a way that it will not rust, accumulate grime or worse yet, dust bunnies?

Safety

Most guns sold in the US include a free safety lock. This is usually some sort of padlock but will vary depending on whether you have a rifle or pistol. Most pistols have a special type of padlock with a cable extension. The idea is to run the cable through the magazine well for semi-automatic pistols or the cylinder for revolvers, and lock it. The locked cable prevents the action or cylinder from closing, thereby rendering the gun safe and inoperable. You can't beat the effectiveness of this system, but it can also be inconvenient if you want to use your gun for home defense.

One of the most popular home storage products is the GunVault. We've been using a GunVault MultiVault for years. The GunVault line is designed to provide security from children and guests. The super-duper nifty part is that GunVaults provide security while still offering near-instant accessibility to your gun.

We're huge fans of GunVault products and here's why.

New guns come with a simple but effective cable lock like this one. You can also get them for free at many gun stores and police stations.

The GunVault handgun safe.

They're designed from the ground up for you, and authorized users designated by you, only, to open easily in the dark. The original model featured a four-finger button combination mechanism. The user sets a pattern of their choice. The buttons are recessed in four finger-sized slots so the combination can be easily entered in the pitch dark. Newer models offer the option of a fingerprint scanner. Just swipe your finger, and the vault opens. The BioMetric (finger-print activated) model stores up to 15 fingerprints, so add fingers from both hands, from your spouse, and anyone else you want to have access. Either method is designed to be foolproof in the middle of the night with no visibility required — it's all done by touch.

The vault door is spring loaded. When you enter the combination or activate the fingerprint scanner, the door springs open in a down-ward direction, allowing access to the vault contents. The interior is foam lined. This not only protects your gun and accessories but helps keep things quiet.

A number of options are available including an interior light, AC and battery power, and low battery indicators. The units all feature mounting holes and security cable attachment points so you can secure the whole vault to the floor, a wall or piece of furniture.

The MultiVault model is the larger version and features a remov-able interior shelf. You can store two handguns or keep a single handgun organized with other valuables, spare magazines or perhaps some secret plans for world domination. If you own one or more handguns, seriously consider getting a GunVault or something func-tionally equivalent to it.

Gun Storage Tips

Don't seal up your guns, let them breathe a bit. Gun cases are great for transport, but not so hot for longer term storage unless you plan to control humidity inside the case. If in doubt, think about how you would or would not store your smartphone for months or years at a time. I'm guessing you wouldn't leave it in the garage or that damp basement, right?

Fingerprints leave a little bit of salty residue on metal. The salt attracts water, which then develops rust. If you plant a nice, juicy thumbprint on a steel gun and leave it, you will eventually see a rust-colored image of your thumb. If you handle your guns, be sure to wipe them down afterward with a rag with some gun oil. You can also find gun cloths already impregnated with silicone or some other metal preservative for the same purpose. If you want to go budget, just find an old cotton t-shirt and sprinkle a very small amount of gun oil around it. Over time, the oil will spread throughout the shirt, and it will become an excellent, and free, way to wipe down your guns.

If you're going to store your guns for a long time, you'll want to wipe them down with a preservative. There are dozens of protectants on the market and just about any one will do for normal storage conditions. Check the retailer's list at the end of this book to find a seller of preservatives.

Store your guns in conditions that you would also store Brown Sugar Cinnamon Pop-Tarts. Not too hot, not too cold, and with relatively normal humidity. If Pop-Tarts will last until their expiration date in your chosen storage area, then your guns should be just fine too.

If your gun is going to be stored, make sure to remove all ammunition. If you keep your gun in a safe, be sure to include a drying agent or even a dehumidifier bar.

PART VIII

RESOURCES

Let's close with some shortcuts to resources that will help you learn and find the extra gear you might need.

WHERE TO BUY ONLINE

IN THE "HOW TO BUY A GUN" section of this book, we discussed the process to buy a gun online.

Of course, there are other reasons to buy a gun online. Large online retailers may have much larger selections in addition to volume prices. Or, some online dealers specialize in rare or antique guns that may not be available locally. There are also auction sites which allow individuals to buy and sell guns through the site. Of course, all interstate transfers have to go through FFL dealers before delivery can take place.

Online Gun Retailers

Gallery Of Guns

Davidson's Inc., the parent of Gallery of Guns, is a gun wholesaler, selling to dealers nationwide. In 1998, Davidson's launched Gallery Of Guns to sell guns direct to consumers through local FFL dealer delivery. Gallery of Guns operates a large catalog website with tens of thousands of new guns from nearly every manufacturer. This is a fantastic way to buy factory new guns. Selection is huge, availability is great, and prices are aggressive. From the time of online purchase, you'll have your gun in a day or two unless your state has mandated waiting periods.

Brownells

Not only does Brownells offer a huge selection of accessories ammo and cleaning and maintenance supplies, they now sell firearms too. As with any other retailer, you buy through their website but complete your background check and pick up the gun at a local dealer.

Auction Sites

You may want to check out GunBroker.com and GunsAmerica.com if you're comfortable with auction sales. Sellers on both sites are a mix of dealers and private sellers. Of course, all firearms need to be shipped to a local dealer so you can complete your background check. Be very careful to study sellers' feedback ratings — we've had mixed results buying from auction sites. Just like eBay, some sellers with high volume can afford to get away with less than ideal service as they have thousands of transactions. You as the buyer only have one feedback, so your comments don't mean much if you have a bad experience.

Online Accessory and Parts Retailers

Brownells — Originally founded as a supplier to gunsmiths, Brownells has grown into a mega-one-stop-shop online retailer. They carry everything. And we mean everything. Accessories, parts, cleaning supplies, safety gear, ammunition, cases, magazines and more. If they don't have it, you probably don't really need it.

Midway USA — Like Brownells, MidwayUSA carries a huge selection of gear, parts, accessories, components, ammunition and more. We've dealt with them for years and years. You have to love how MidwayUSA supports the NRA and other shooting institutions. One last thing — be sure to check out the Clearance link on the home page from time to time. You never know what you'll find there, and the deals are great.

Online Ammunition Retailers

It's easy to buy ammunition online. Most states allow you to purchase from online sources. But don't worry, these ammunition retailers will know the rules and whether they can legally ship to you. Even with shipping costs factored in, you might save a few bucks and benefit from big selections of available stock. If you don't see a retailer on this list, don't worry. These are just some of the ones where we've gotten great customer service over the years.

Brownells — Brownells entered the online ammunition business in the same manner they do everything else — with major attention to detail and customer service. We've never gone wrong buying anything from Brownells.

LuckyGunner.com — LuckyGunner has invested in a fantastic online inventory system that only shows items that are in stock and ready for immediate shipment. If you see it on the website, it will ship immediately — usually on the same day. Prices are excellent, and service is stellar.

MidSouth Shooters Supply — Another longstanding general purpose retailer. You'll find ammunition, reloading supplies, shooting accessories and more at MidSouth.

Able's — Yet another general shooting supply retailer, Able's carries just about anything you need for hunting and general purpose shooting.

TJ Conevera — TJ Conevera focuses on reloading components, and they do a stellar job of shipping products immediately. You also have to work pretty hard to find better prices. We can't recommend them highly enough.

TRAINING, DEALERS AND SHOOTING RANGES

Online Training Resources

NSSF Videos — The National Shooting Sports Foundation operates a YouTube channel filled with tutorial videos. You can also subscribe to the NSSF Podcast for videos.

Brownells — You've got to check out the Brownells video library. They constantly produce quality videos with tips on gun cleaning, accessorizing and maintenance. Great stuff!

Training Programs

National Shooting Sports Foundation First Shots Program — Learn to shoot at a First Shots seminar near you!

National Rifles Association Safety Programs — Find a National Rifle Association safety class near you.

Thunder Ranch — Ready for some first-rate training combined with real hospitality? Book early. Really early!

GunSite Academy — One of the most established shooting schools, you can't go wrong here.

RangeMaster — If you live in the eastern half of the US, check out RangeMaster. Tom and Lynn Givens and staff provide outstanding self-defense training.

Shootrite Training Academy — For the armed citizen Shootrite develops the mental and physical skills to defend self and family, whether it's through avoidance and escape or the actual act of fighting. Shootrite's priorities are safety, developing effective fighting skills, and creating the mindset and confidence required for victory in violent situations.

Shooting Ranges

WhereToShoot.org — Find shooting ranges near you.

COMPETITIVE SHOOTING

ONE OF THE best ways to become a better shooter is to get involved with some local competitions. They are generally low-key, low-stress and high-fun. Never done one? No worries, just show up for a match. There will almost certainly be a new shooter orientation, and if not, experienced shooters will be more than happy to help you.

Competitive shooting won't teach you combat or self-defense strategies, but it's a great way to learn how to operate your gun under a little bit of stress. When your gun goes "click" while the clock is running, you'll get quite adept at your malfunction routines!

International Defensive Pistol Association — Compete with "semi-realistic" self-defense scenarios. It's a great way to get in some fun practice with your carry or home-defense gun.

Single Action Shooting Society — Yes, this is cowboy action shooting. Can you say pure fun? Lotsa old-style guns and competitors that call themselves names like Evil Roy, Black Bearded Bert, and Molly Misfire.

Steel Challenge Shooting Association — Lots of rounds down-range as fast as you can pull the trigger. You'll draw and shoot at steel plates and learn to love that satisfying "clang."

United States Practical Shooting Association — The ultimate in run and gun. USPSA is all about lots of shooting, moving and speed. You'll see space-age race guns, but don't worry, there are classes where all competitors use stock equipment — like the gun you just bought!

LEGAL STUFF AND RESOURCES

IN THIS COUNTRY, the excuse of "not knowing the law" doesn't get you very far. So while we're including some links to resources to help you understand gun laws, you are always solely responsible for understanding local laws and regulations in your area. While "I don't recall" seems to be a perfectly acceptable defense strategy for elected officials, that plan doesn't work so well for us ordinary citizens.

Gun Laws Websites

United States Concealed Carry Association

The USCCA offers a wealth of free and paid information on everything self-defense related. Videos, books, articles are available on a free and paid basis. You also might check out their personal defense liability plans if you intend to use a gun for protection.

USA Carry

USA Carry was founded in 2007 as a resource to help concealed carriers understand state by state carry permits. It has since grown to a large community of over 50,000 forum users. The site includes concealed carry maps that show concealed carry permit reciprocity and state by state gun law summaries. USA Carry also includes directories of shooting instructors and gun ranges.

HandGunLaw.us

This site focuses on state-by-state gun laws and concealed carry permit reciprocity. If you want to know where your states' permit is valid, check here. Each state has a printable PDF document that summarizes gun laws. Better yet, the documents link directly to state statutes so you can see the raw legalese yourself.

NRA Institute for Legislative Action

It's worth spending some time exploring the NRA.org main site. From there you'll find the NRA-ILA web site which contains mountains of information on various state laws, recent legal challenges and relevant gun law articles from around the country.

PARTING SHOTS

WE HOPE you enjoyed reading this book. It's intended to help relieve some of the apprehension and stress to finding, buying and shooting guns safely.

Most importantly, pay attention to the safety tips. Shooting is an incredibly safe pastime when people faithfully obey the four rules of gun safety.

One last thing. Your reviews on the retail site where you purchased this book are incredibly important to authors like me. If you found value in the book, I would greatly appreciate you leaving a review. If you didn't enjoy the book, how about dropping me an email to let me know how to make the next edition better?

Now go have fun and be safe!

ABOUT THE AUTHOR

Tom McHale is a committed learning junkie always seeking a new subject victim. As a lifelong student of whatever grabs his attention on any particular day, he thrives on beating rabbit trails into submission. In between his time as a high-tech marketing executive, restaurant owner, and hamster cosmetology practitioner, he's published seven books and nearly 1,500 articles.

For Tom, learning is only half the fun — the other half is sharing his experiences with readers using his trademark "half-cocked but right on target" style.

Feel free to visit Tom at his website, MyGunCulture.com. It's a half-cocked but right on target look at the world of shooting and all things related. If you want to learn with a laugh about guns, shooting products, personal defense, competition, industry news and the occasional Second Amendment issue, visit him there.

Follow Tom online:

www.mygunculture.com

tom@practical-guides.com

ALSO BY TOM MCHALE

CPSIA information can be obtained
at www.ICGtesting.com
Printed in the USA
LVHW041113081218
599746LV00021B/547/P